FEATHERS AND FLUTTERS FROM THE CROW'S NEST

KAREN CROW

First printing 2008

Printed in the United States

ISBN# 978-0-9815203-1-5

Truth Book Publishers
Franklin, Illinois
www.truthbookpublishers.com

Dedication

Why Do I Write?

Chapters :

This book of poems, feelings and thoughts is dedicated to my four grandparents, my parents, and family. Their love, guidance, and instruction have made me the person I am today.

Each member has touched my life and influenced me in a very special way. My memories are precious and forever a part of me. Thanks to the Lord who has protected me in times of disappointment. He sustains me in times of trouble.

He is my shield and the lifter of my head.

Why do I write?

Why do I love to write?
Let me count the ways.
The beauty I see and the feelings I have
    can be listed all of my days.
Every experience of my life has left its
    mark on me.
The joys and the sorrows make their
    difference, even to the friends I see.
The sunset and sunrise of each day bring
    color to my life.
Each trouble and trail is lessened with the
    beauty of each strife.
If I can lighten the load of a co-worker in
    some way, it has been all good.
When I think of others first, I am doing
    what I should.
Blow over me winds of laughter, joy and
    peace.
Make my heart glad and my days merry
    until my life shall cease.

The American Crow

The American Crow

Did you know that the Crow is the most intelligent bird, with the largest brain? The Crow is completely black, 21 inches long, with a fan-shaped tail and a wingspread of three feet. The Crow can perform synonymous functions and make complex decisions. They can even match black dots on a set of five boxes with the number of objects on each box. Crows can be easily tamed and can mimic some human sounds.

Crows mate in late winter. The males and females build the foot-wide nest together. They take turns incubating the three to seven eggs. Both parents feed the nestlings. Young Crows fledge (leave the nest) after five weeks.

While feeding, one or two Crows will be the lookout on top of a tall tree, sending an alarm to other Crows that are feeding. They live everywhere—woods, parks, fields, riversides, towns.

Crows destroy many harmful insects and rodents. They lead wolves and coyotes to a carcass to open it—doing the work for them, making the meat more accessible. While cleaning up dead animals and road kill, they help with the spread of disease and bacteria.

Crows gather in groups of up to eight during the summer. In winter, they gather in larger groups from miles around. Thousands of Crows may roost together. A flock of Crows is a "murder."

Crows do not get along with birds of prey such as hawks, owls and eagles. They will mob these birds by dive-bombing, chasing or harassing them.

"All in all, Crows are very family-oriented birds. They are an example of how to live as a family, protecting one another, being loyal in every way. Crows are very social creatures."

1

Precious Family

Harvey, my Partner

You are my steadfast partner in life.
You remain true through all the strife.
Even though I don't always feel your love, I know it is there.
I pray I will be a partner who is willing to share.
Life has thrown us some curves we didn't expect.
Thank the Lord, His love and care we did not reject.
The years have flown by and we have missed so much.
I pray for your understanding and your tender touch.

My Children

My children, I love you. You mean so much to me.
I'm thankful for the gifts God has given me in you.
You make me proud and happy, as part of your life I can be.
I pray I have been the example I should be, tried and true.
There is nothing in this world I wouldn't do to make your life complete.
My heart is with you in all your trials and endeavors.
Praise God, when you leave this world, your Savior you will meet.
I'm so proud of all three of you; you are precious treasures.

Grandchildren of Mine

Grandchildren, you are gifts from heaven above.
You are so special. Each one of you, I dearly love.
God made you all so very unique and beautiful, too.
Your intelligence amazes me. Your worth is countless to measure; it is true.
May God richly bless each one of you, in whatever you strive to do.
You are such blessings. I love all eight of you!

Deputy Crow – MG24

Harvey, the Morgan County Deputy, we are so proud of
   you.
In order to successfully complete your job duties, there was
   almost nothing you wouldn't do.
You didn't even notice your daughter waving at you, while
   driving down Morton Avenue.
It must be that you were thinking about where you were
   headed next, until your day was through.

Thanks to Sheriff Johnson for hiring you and to Sheriff Roberts
   for his kindness in keeping you on the Force.
In every position you have served—correctional officer, court
   security & bailiff, and civil processor—you have completed
   your job well, of course!
Harv decided to order business cards to leave on the doors
   to save trips and the county some money.
Sally mentioned this at a seminar to other civil processors;
   she wasn't proud of this "Hound Dog" any!

In each café in town, a former prisoner will yell from the
   kitchen window, "Hi, Harv!" to repay his respect.
Deputy Crow became acquainted with the office personnel
   of many businesses, as you might expect.
A worker at Passavant Hospital once told Harvey he was a
   nice guy —for a cop!
That was such a compliment. His caring ways and kind heart
   will probably never stop.

Deputy Crow (continued)

One day his wife went to the office to ask Harv for a lunch date.
Pat Taylor said, "Oh, he just went out with Edna,"
(Langdon, you see!)
They must have gone to Steak 'n' Shake, CRs, or Shooters.
Where else could they possibly be?
We won't forget the day he tried to save some embarrassment
and became a "drive-through" cop.
What about the man in the semi who saw Harv coming, drove
backwards across the field and didn't stop?

Harvey will miss his County friends and the work he faithfully
did there.
He'll probably even miss the trips to St. Charles, Dwight,
Blessing Hospital, McFarland, Hillsboro, Chester, even
Dallas, TX, and the meals with Ed and friends that he did
share.
He won't miss taking babies out of one parent's arms to give to
another.
He'll remember the eviction papers, the little girl home alone,
and asking the landlord, "Can we wait till Monday to give
this paper to her Mother?"

When Harvey began this journey, he really didn't know if he
could fill the shoes of a deputy.
His dedication, respect for others and love of the Lord helped
him to accomplish each task completely.
Now it's time to hunt and fish and maybe some part-time
farming, too.
Happy Retirement, Harvey! We wish the very best to you.

Love, Karen and your County Friends

<u>10 things I remember about my Mother,</u>
Frances Marie Vedder

**She was a Christian.
She taught Sunday School as a teenager.
I could pray with her about anything.
She and Dad took me to Band practices,
parades, & trips.
She was talented in English/Composition.
She gave me my talent to rhyme/write
poetry.
She kept her house clean.
She was great at creating good menus.
Matching colors/clothes was one of her
talents.
She was not given the credit/love she
deserved as a child.**

Jesus, my Savior

Jesus, I love you. I know thou art mine.
All my life I will praise you. You are all divine.
How can I thank you for what you've done for me?
When I need a friend, you are there, for none other can I see.
You are worthy of all glory, honor and praise.
I will love and thank you all of my days.

This is my Dad: Charles Thomas Mutch

Dad, you are so special. I have many things to thank you for.
You have always been there for me—never turning your back or
    shutting the door.
You are very giving and not afraid to speak your mind.
Yet, you always know the truth and how to be loving and kind.
Protection and support you have given your sister, Aunt
    Marjorie.
You answered the call of duty as a veteran of WWII,
    loving your country.

Years ago, down in the bottoms, I was headed for the creek on a
    wagon of corn.
My screaming didn't help a bit, but you caught that team of
    horses and wagon just in time—before they could do me any
    harm.
You've worked hard all your life and took on the responsibility
    of the family farm.
You could back a truck or a wagon with such ease and charm.

You and Mother were always there, making sure Charla and I
    attended all functions of the Jacksonville High School Band.
It was a wonderful experience. After receiving the John Philip
    Souza Award, we really should have given our folks a hand.
Your love of basketball is evident, as you purchased those season
    tickets each year.
I remember a "Crow" boy who played at Murrayville Grade
    School, whom you supported and gave many a cheer.

You asked Harvey to farm with you and treated him like a son.
I thank you for what you have sacrificed for us. Life on the farm
    was the best—along with the trials and the fun.
I appreciate the gift of the International "B."
It brings back happy memories—the likes we will never again see.

Whether it was wallpapering and painting our first home "down
    on the hill," moving many times, or building our brick
    home, you always did your part and more.
As a member of Calvary Baptist Church, you've had many
    positions and been the preacher's right-hand man—from
    the very start!
You've chauffeured many an older member to church and
    started a handicapped class when they said it couldn't be
    done.
Your laughter and uplifting spirit have made many a problem
    get up and run!

Your gift of intuition is very valuable to our family.
Not only did it tell you to "check the gap or gate," it saved the
    lives of Kirby and me.
When you enlisted the neighbors and started digging, it got us
    out of the snow.
You really were "right on" because when I had my first pain, we
    didn't have far to go.

Enjoy your life and take care in your traveling to and fro.
Slow down, or you will have to buy new runners for your walker,
    so you can go, go, go!
With your counseling skills, you helped the self-esteem of several
    of your friends.
You sat with shut-in neighbors and took others to the doctor.
    Your commitment never ends!

We love you, Father Dear. You're thought of most fondly on this
    your 80th Birthday, and every day throughout the year!

Dothia Annabelle Crow

Memories of you will never fade.
Even now, we can taste your delicious
  homemade bread, sugar cookies and
  pies that you so frequently made.

Your determination and steadfastness
  were inspirations to your family.
'Open arms' for all your grandchildren,
  made each of them love you more
  dearly.

When illness came your way, you didn't
  give up or quit.
Instead you drove your Blue Chevy Malibu
  and lived a full life in spite of it!

Thanks for keeping us in school, giving
  us piano lessons, encouraging us to
  practice and for always being there.
You loved your children and grandchildren
  equally, with plenty of love to share.

You were proud of your class ring and
  graduating with the Class of 1927!
Just remembering you in your glider,
  straw hat and apron, with your sweet
  smile, makes us feel a little closer to
  heaven.

The WLDS Daily News at 9:00 AM and
4:30 PM, you never wanted to miss.
Your favorite color was 'pink' and
Waddell's was where you shopped
for that new dress!

You loved having your hair combed and
eating ice cream.
Yes, your flower bed and roses were
beautiful, but not as beautiful as
the memory of you.

Kerry

Kerry is a good-looking man, with a
  smile that will melt your heart.
He is a good father—and has been
  from the start!

Tenderhearted and likable are traits
  he has shown.
He would give a friend anything he
  owns.

When a problem arises on any given
  day.
Kerry has ingenuity and will always
  figure out a way.

Playing trombone and country dancing
  are talents he has been given.
When he's coming down the track at a
  tractor pull, he's in heaven!

When he was a little boy, a job of raking
  leaves for Great-Grandpa Shorty
  produced a dollar.
Grandpa said to share with his brother,
  so he tore it in two without a little
  bother!

Kerry

Kerry, you are fun loving with a smile that will melt your heart.
You are a wonderful father—and it has been so from the start!

Tenderhearted and friendly are traits you have always shown.
You would give anyone the shirt off your back or anything else
you own.
Evan Donellson was thankful for the ball glove you gave him.
Those Mexican friends liked the donuts and Coke, setting a kind
tone.

When a problem arises, you have ingenuity and can figure out a way.
You made a garden tractor from scratch. What else can we say?

Playing trombone and country line dancing are talents you were
given.
You enjoyed those tractor pulls. Winning seemed a little like
heaven.

Remember the leaf-raking job offered by Grandpa Shorty for a
dollar?
"Share with your brother," he said. You tore it in two—no bother.

Only you could get on "Babe." Your love for animals came through.
Two raccoons rested on your back; and when your Dad killed the
puppies, you asked, "What will their mommy do?"

Farming and truck driving are indeed professions you know well.
Receiving the "Best Backing" award in FFA has been proven, as
anyone can tell.

You love your family, home and country. It is certainly true!
Your trust in the Lord and speaking the "right" will surely bring
blessings to you.

Kirby

Kirby is well-liked and thought of
    fondly by all his friends.
He's a hard worker, who works long
    hours to tie up all ends.

A more organized man you will
    never find.
Kirby is definitely the dependable
    kind.

His motto is "Don't waste daylight
    hours" of the day.
In making money, he can always
    figure out a way!

He was a truck driver, 'snowbird,'
    and now works for the state
    of Illinois.
A better husband you'll never meet.
    He fills his children's hearts
    with joy.

Kirby is always determined to
    finish the job whether building
    a home or a three-level deck.
If there's a job to do, Kirby will
    tackle it, by heck!

KIRBY

Kirby, you are so special, as you have always been to us.
Your name means "from the church village" or, clearly, one you can trust.
You were called "blizzard" or "snowball" because of your miraculous birth that snowy January day.
"Don't waste daylight hours," you have been heard to say.
It seems that, even in Bible School, your organizational skills were easy to see.
Dedicated and true to a worthy cause—you will always be!
As a child you were usually clowning around, but could be counted on to do your part.
Your love and closeness to family could be seen from the very start.
Early in the morning we could hear you in the rocking chair, while watching the Lone Ranger on TV.
That chair would move across the room, closer to the screen, so all the action you could see.
You once asked your Grandma, "Do soldiers really die?"
She told you the story of the soldier's Bible in his pocket, hiding a bullet from his heart, with a sigh.
Dependable you are, as needed, to finish any task.
Doing the job is all that's important. Questions you seldom ask.
Doing a "wheelie" is no problem, with your front tire upward bound.
You can ski on a mountain, but want to keep your feet on the ground.
Dedication is the key word to your trucking career, which you proved for many years.
That word applies to you as a state employee; for hard work and loyalty, you have no fears.
"Cleanliness is next to godliness" must be true.
Why? Because a bucket, soap and a rag sure seem to be natural to you!
Loving and providing for your family is foremost in your heart.
Respect and pride for you—from us will never part!

16

Kyla

Kyla is so beautiful. By God, she
  has been blest.
She is quick to learn, as Master
  technician, she passed Capitals'
  test.

Kyla is lovable and to the point.
Even when a little girl, she said,
  "I don't want to talk about it
  anymore."
She's a diligent housekeeper and
  cleaned Max's feet at the door.

She is a loyal friend and has many—
  old and new.
When they need her, there's nothing
  she wouldn't do!

Her talents are many—singing, dancing,
  decorating. She was an asset to
  two western-wear stores.
Kyla is fast with her hands. Whether
  mechanical or instructional, she
  can handle any and all chores.

She loves her brothers, nieces and
  nephews and worries about her
  Mom and Dad.
Kyla, what a daughter! A better one
  we could never have had!

KYLA HARVETTE

Kyla, you are so special, our little girl, sent to us by God.
Your name means "beautiful one." Through some heartache your feet
have trod. It doesn't take one long to see that you really care.
With your friends, love, loyalty and kindness you do share.

As a little girl, you weren't able to go on the trip to Florida and accepted it so
graciously. You unpacked your suitcase and said, "let's don't talk about it
anymore," so bravely. The love and respect you have for us, as your parents,
are very easy to see. God gave you an inner beauty. He knew what a fine
lady you would be.

Mother will never forget your thoughtfulness on her birthday and every
Mother's Day. You would make a purchase at Mason's Grocery because it
was all you could pay.
It was always very obvious that you are loyal to your friends. Admiration for
you from the mothers of your childhood friends will never end.

The flowers you planted at the Rea Place were mowed down by a cousin, so
what could we do? You would play in the garden with your cars, making
roads to Murrayville and Nortonville, too.
Kept so neatly in your always rearranged, pink room was Raggedy Ann and
Andy. Digging up Grandma Crow's pink roses was simple, because you are
so handy!

The disappointments that have touched your life have only made you strong.
You never let them get you down, even though the road may be long.
It never ceases to amaze me how you can smile through so much adversity.
God gave you a strong constitution, willing heart, work ethic, and "it will be
all right" ability.

The talents you possess are many—from singing and customer service to
sensitivity of heart.
Even though life has not always been easy, determination was evident from
the start.
You are blessed with your partner, Jim, who is a kind, loving, intelligent
man.
Your desire for a child was fulfilled in Cheney Annabelle, by God's gracious
plan.

May God continue to bless you and hold you in the palm of His hand.
No weapon formed against you will be able to stand.

"divide the attention"

Share your love with your children. Each
one needs special care for his/her
every thought and concern.
Every child is special and "one of a kind."
God knew us even before we were born.
Every hair on our head is numbered. That
makes us pretty unique!
We were made in the image of God.

Our children are gifts from God. We must
untie the packages carefully. We hold that
precious gift up and look at it, admiringly.
We say thank you. We take special pride
in it. We clean it. We show it off. We
protect it lovingly.
Such innocence deserves our closest attention.
We must rescue them when they fall or
stumble.

Our Lord rescues us from the cradle to the
grave.

To my daughter-in-law:
Shawn

Shawn is always upbeat and wears a great big smile.
Her hair is blonde, which looks just great in any style.
Decorating is a talent she demonstrates with such flair.
She got out the brush, painted the wall again—I declare!
Shawn's love of scrapbooking is easy to see.
A book of party photos she presented to Harvey and to me.
When you need help to move, clean out a shed, or have a sale, she is there.
Whether giving of her time or a ride to therapy, her love she will share.
Making models from impressions is a worthwhile profession to possess.
This lady has a bounce to her step and completes life's duties with finesse.

To my daughter-in-law:
Michelle

Michelle is quick-witted, intelligent and so funny.
When in a party group, her comments are right on the money.
Her childhood memories are special because of her dear 'Opal Emmaline.'
This grandmother instilled love and support at all times.
Michelle grew up independent and teaches to her children this quality.
Homework is so important to their future, don't you see?
She travels to and fro from sports to band events with punctuality.
At FS her duties are varied, but don't forget her 'training' ability.
Michelle doesn't need to buy a star. She made one for her wall.
Small as a "twig" you say? But not easily bent; she stands tall.

Jim Brewer

What a son-in-law are you!
When it comes to helping others, there isn't anything you won't do.
You clean smokehouses and can make a nice fire.
Helping mow the neighbor's yard is easy for you—and not for hire!
You have added so much to our family—your smile and listening ear.
You always have a way of filling many hearts with cheer.
Doing your job at EMI is a dedication others know.
They all want to work for you because purpose and kindness you always show.
Camping is a happy get-away for you and your family.
Just sitting around a campfire, visiting old and new friends—true you will always be!
Your dreams for the future can become a reality.
With your proactive thoughts and actions, hello retirement and RV—just wait and see!
Set your mind on things above and He will see you through.
With your smile, love and devotion, there is nothing you cannot do!

(Jim is now owner of Brewer Trucking.)

SETH MICHAEL

Seth, you are so brave. You have been since the age of two.
All the Crows love you and think the best of you.
You have a heart and know what's right and wrong.
You played alto sax and trumpet on any band song.
There is no one I am prouder of than you, Seth.
You have made the most of your situation and all the rest.
I can imagine, at times, the emptiness you may have felt.
You have made the best of the life you have been dealt.
But God has a plan for you; He's your Heavenly Father.
Turn to Him; He'll guide you like no other.
Please, don't give up on life. There is a reason for each day.
Your pain and hurt has helped you grow. He knows the way.
God makes the things meant for bad, to turn to good for you, eventually.
Don't let anything stop your hopes. Don't give up! I say, prayerfully.

Caulyn Turner

Caulyn is a fine grandson who is easy-going and calm.

His hobby of shooting clay pigeons is a very talented one.

As a sure shot, money and prizes he has won.

You can see him riding his motorcycle almost any nice day.

He even mastered "wheelies" in his father's stylish way.

The nickname "Duke" is appropriate with his steady personality.

He manages his finances quite well and is very thrifty.

Caulyn has always been a good student—writing his thoughts, too.

With his determination, there is nothing he cannot do.

21

Evan Layne

Evan is such a gentle young man. His character is unsurpassed.
He is willing to assist anyone and dedicated to each task.
One of his many talents is playing the alto saxophone.
While riding his International tractor, he seems to enjoy the time alone.

Evan is a great student and a hard worker at sports, at home, or at school.
Whether playing baseball, basketball, or football, he knows the rules.
He listens and learns while conversing with adults and the respect is mutual you see.
Evan is always thankful, can help stain your deck and then politely
ask for some sweet tea.

Cassidy Dayne

Second to none is Cassidy. She is a first-class kind of girl.
Her style is natural, poised, patient and easy-going, too.
Cassi loves horses and gave At-a-Girl gate-jumping lessons a whirl.
She showed her first heifer at the county fair like a pro, it's true.

Her talents are many as you would agree.
Adding a verse to a song at church was no trouble for her.
Cassi can model clothes and her true self you will see.
She enjoys a group dance at school or the dance studio—for sure.

There is no better baby-sitter that could be found than Cassidy.
Caring for her two younger sisters is a duty Cassi doesn't shirk.
Her love is seen while saying "Is there anything else you need from me?"
Caring for others and her sensitive heart could be a sign from God
regarding her life's work.

Kable Gayle

Kable is our granddaughter with a great big beautiful smile.
Each day she says, "This is the best day of my life," smiling all the while.
She loves to drive her red golf cart, giving her cousins and friends a ride.
Each one enjoys a tour of the farm with Kable showing the countryside with pride.

To say that Kable is a great dancer is an understatement, you see.
She has traveled to New York with Dance Company.
Flying is no problem for her. It's just another great day to live.
With her attitude and good philosophy of life, Kable has so much to give.

Carsyn RaeAnne

Carsyn is almost 3 years old and quite a personality is she.

Her sweet smile and great big eyes are mesmerizing to see.

She always say "Hi" to Grandma and Grandpa so respectfully.

Carsyn loves to talk and expresses herself so sweetly.

This little girl has a mind of her own and really enjoys life.

Prophesy states some day she will be a preacher's wife.

23

Bretlyn Emmaline

Bretlyn is so precious; she dances to the beat!
Her smile and ways are angelic. May God guide her little feet.

Contentment is a virtue difficult to attain.
Bretlyn Emmaline manages this with ease.
She loves to eat and walk around and never does complain.
Whatever comes across her path, I pray, Dear Lord, just cover
her, watch over her, would you please?

She gazes with amazement at what is before her eyes.
She takes it all in—whatever the scene.
It doesn't matter what happens, she can handle it.
She always tries.
As a granddaughter, she's such a pleasure.
I believe she's a prayer answered and a living little dream.

(This was written when Bretlyn was a toddler.
The words hold true today.)

An addition must be made which is Bret's quick wit.
She is so intelligent that her imagination just does not quit.

Cheney Annabelle

What a blessing is Cheney Annabelle. She is sensitive, kind, and caring too.

Cheney doesn't hesitate to show her feelings or to say "I love you."

She longed for a playmate. A brother or sister would do, you know.

But just in time, the school bus picked her up and to Kindergarten she did go.

This little girl makes friends wherever she may be.

She loves to dance and tumble and is quite expressive, you see.

Playing alone is OK, but when her cousins arrive, she is in heaven.

Cheney understands many things even though she is not even seven.

Praying comes natural for her. She says, "Let's pray," with friends or at home.

A little child shall lead them, says the Bible. May Cheney's sweet spirit never roam.

She goes to her Great-grandfather's grave, kisses her hand and then touches the stone.

May the Good Lord bless her. He says He will never leave us alone.

"but I'm not going to cry"

A sweet, four-year old grandson says to his cousin (who is looking out the window for his mommy and daddy), "He wants his daddy and mommy." "I want my daddy and mommy, too, but I'm not going to cry."

The year-old grandson has both parents living with him. The four-year old grandson is a product of divorce at age two. Shortly after the divorce, he walked across the yard toward the only home he knew. He was told by his grandmother and his aunt, "Nobody is home there any more." He walked with determination and said, "I want to go home."

We must all go home sometime. Home could be back to our roots or our home place. Home could be "accepting our situation." Home could be traveling to our parents, our family for the holidays or while on vacation.

Home is security, safety from the storm, being with family who loves us. Home is a haven of rest from a weary day's work. Home is a shelter from the storm.

Home will eventually be "home" with the Lord. Home is being with our Savior for eternity, where there will be no more sorrow, sickness, night or death. Little boys will hurt no more.

HOME SWEET HOME.

Caulyn's Deer Caper

The fine hunter, Caulyn Crow, shot a deer on the other side of the creek, you know.
He couldn't get it out, so what did he do, he called Grandpa Crow.
The old Toyota, 4-wheel-drive was just what he needed for his deer.
Harv asked, "Where are you going to take it?" To a friend's house, said Caulyn. So Grandpa said, "We'll take you there."

They had never been down this road. The brakes were dragging and they almost got in the ditch because Grandpa was going pretty fast.
They passed the friend's lane, down the bumpy hill, to the bottom, at last.
They turned around. Up the hill they went, bump, bump all the way.
They found the lane, so they could deliver Caulyn's deer without delay.

The friend said, "What do you have for me?" Caulyn said, "I shot a deer and brought it to you."
What a nice gesture for a friend to do.
When they looked in the back of the truck, Kirby said, "Heck, it's not in the truck." No deer could they see.
"We'll be right back," said Grandpa, knowing right where the deer might be.

Out the drive they went and down the road, bump, bump.
Sure enough, lying in the middle of the road, was the deer they didn't mean to dump.
The moral of this story is—You should have a <u>tailgate</u> and take a <u>light</u> to pen on your deer!

My Sister, Charla

There is a spunky lady who lives in Florida—Coral Springs.
She is determined to succeed and with the Lord's help,
   she has done all things.

As Mother, she sacrifices for her family.
"I need tires—shoes—tuition. I'm moving back home."
   "OK, I'll close in the patio. Yes, siree!"

Her detective skills are evident—as she can climb that wall,
   watch from a car's darkened windows, or find the
   combination in no time!
As secretary at Coldwell Banker, addition of her boss's
   duties—she handles just fine!

Charla is pretty, petite and tan.
She can dance and romance, and fry up bacon in a pan!

She understands your hurts and is willing to lend a listening ear.
Charla, my sister, my friend, you fill my heart with cheer!

Charla & Bob

To Mr. and Mrs. Bob Hayes. . . .
A happier couple there could never be.
In my heart, Charla has a special place.
She is my little sister; don't you see?

God was watching over both of you.
His love brought you together at the perfect time.
Without each other, you would have been so very blue.
Now as husband and wife, your lives are joyfully entwined.

Branson Fall Vacation 1999

What a great time it was! The likes of it, you will never see.
Those in the "Mutch" mobile were Dad, Harvey, Charla and me.

From beginning to end, everything worked out swell—even when
　　we stopped to eat and just relaxed a spell.
The accommodations at The Plantation at Fall Creek were very
　　comfortable and made us feel right at home.
We saw many sights; all over Branson we did roam.

Shoji Tabuchi was an excellent show; such a great talent is he!
We drove to Table Rock Dam and toured the fish hatchery.
The Bobby Vinton Show brought back many memories of days
　　gone by.
Stopping at an occasional shop was OK, but it made Dad and
　　Harvey give a sigh!

On top of the Inspirational Tower you could see the countryside
　　for miles around, with all its beauty.
The clouds rolled back and the sun did shine, and we headed for
　　Silver Dollar City.
You should have seen the look on Dad's face when he got his
　　instructions and started off on the motorized cart!
We knew we were in for some fun—right from the very start.

There was a comedy team on Main Street, with specialty shops
　　to see. When Dad came near that $165 vase, oh dear me!
But, the most fun for Charla and I was riding backwards on the
　　Thunderbolt . . . . whee!
Yakov Smirnoff was so patriotic and funny. We really enjoyed
　　his show.
We had to eat that 'pulled-pork sandwich' at Shorty Small's'; so
　　off we did go.

The final show was Mickey Gilley, with his great comedian. We
　　laughed, and laughed; it was medicine to our soul.
We were leaving behind all the fun, but the memories
　　still grow and grow.
The trip home to Illinois, which lost its 's,' seemed rather long.
Branson, you gave us a special lift and filled our hearts with a song!

30

What my Grandparents Did for Me

What does it mean to have loving grandparents? It means everything in the world. Just remembering them and how they made me feel, helping me to know that life is worthwhile—even when we grow old. The wisdom they shared with me was so powerful. One grandfather said, "I don't worry about the things I have no control over. It's the things I can do something about and don't do that worries me." My other grandfather said, "Be sweet," and "You must repent. You can't just be saved and then do anything you choose. You must answer for what you do."

The excitement of visiting my grandparents was always the same. I can even feel it now. One grandmother always cooked rice for me for supper—with sugar and cream. Ymmm! My other Grandmother never failed to have bananas on top of the refrigerator and plenty of longhorn cheese inside—and I could always eat all I wanted to. One grandmother always bought something for everyone for Christmas—from her children to her great-grandchildren. My other grandmother offered to baby-sit with my two little boys, even when her health was failing.

There was peace in the homes of my grandparents. I felt safe and loved.

One grandmother taught me how to can peaches and tomatoes. She also introduced me to a love of music and the fascination of the sound of harmony. My sister and I loved to sing while Grandmother was playing on Sunday afternoon. We learned to sing harmony on those days, with Grandma's fingers flowing gracefully over those keys. It was so much fun!! As time passed,

31

grandmother's hands shook and she could not play when we asked her to. My other grandmother taught me how to make baby quilts by hand from old sheet blankets. She also showed me how to clean windows with vinegar and water for a sparkling, squeaky-clean shine.

Grandparents have time for their grandchildren and life never seems rushed. They take them for long rides; get them some ice cream; and take them to old-fashioned movies in the park, sitting on a bench. My memories of either set of grandparents driving in our parent's driveway, sitting for a while in lawn chairs in the yard, having some iced tea and then going on their way home will forever be a very happy thought.

Both my grandmothers were great workers in the community. If there was a need, they both were there to help. If there was a sickness, a group of ladies would clean their neighbor's house. If there was a death, my grandmothers could easily do what had to be done for the family, without asking any questions.

When I get to heaven, I want to see Jesus first; then, I want to look for my precious grandparents.

As I touch the lives of my grandchildren, I want to remember what an impression my grandparents made on me. I realize that the influence, love and telling of the gospel, is very important to a young, soft heart. If I can leave nothing more than the true meaning of life, I will have left them everything. The things of this world will all fade away, but the words of eternal life will remain forever. If I haven't left something that cannot be bought, I really have left nothing worth leaving. God help me to treasure the good gifts and pass them on to my family.

"Be Sweet"

"Be Sweet," my Grandpa Orvel Mutch used to say, when I visited him.
Every time I started to get in my car, he repeated this "sweet" phrase.
That ....I thought I would always be. It didn't seem so difficult to do.
Little did I know, life would turn sour.
Its bitterness would soon emanate from my lips.
Resentment was flowing from my heart.
I was not that sweet little girl anymore.
I was feeling things I never thought I would ever feel.
The circumstances of life produced disappointments, broken dreams
   and changes in relationships.
This turn of events turned a "sweet" girl sour.

The issue is not the circumstances.
The issue is how I handled them.
Bitterness and resentment began to emerge from a once, sweet soul.
The pieces of broken dreams are easier to put into the puzzle.
Those pieces of broken relationships don't seem to fit.

The only healing is a departure from unforgiveness.
Forgiveness was possible through the grace of God—not in my own might.
There is an egress, or way out.
His name is Jesus.

Thank you, Lord. I am on my way to "sweetness" again.

Grandmother Beulah

Loving and so supportive was my Grandmother Beulah to me.
Helping her neighbors during times of sickness and death
was a passion of hers, you see.
Supper would be ready and chores all done when grandfather came home
from a day's work.
Caring for her developmentally-disabled daughter was a duty she did not shirk.
This Christian lady sang like an angel at church and funerals with perfect ease.
Her piano playing was eagerly anticipated after Sunday dinner,
as it flowed so beautifully.
She taught me the art of canning peaches and tomatoes, which was merely a part
of her cooking ability.
Grandmother was understanding of my concerns and hurts and let me know
that she cared.
Baby-sitting with my two little boys was a precious memory
of the love she shared.

Why worry?

"I don't worry about the things I can do nothing about.
It's the things I can do something about, and don't,
that worry me."

           --Grandpa Frank Vedder

What wise counsel our grandparents convey to us!
When Grandpa backed into the tree by his driveway,
    he said, "When did they put that tree there?"
We have little control over most happenings in life.
      However . . . . .
      We can pray!
      We can forgive!
      We can say a kind word!
      We can be the feet of someone who has none.
      We can give of our time, our money and our
          talents.
      We can assist those who are less fortunate
          than ourselves.
      We can lay hands on the sick, the hurting.
      We can rebuke the devil from our families.
      We can gather together with believers to worship.
      We can PRAISE the LORD!
Thank you, Lord, that I don't have to worry.
YOU ARE IN CONTROL.
Praise your name!

Grandma Lula Belle

Grandma Vedder was very attractive. She was a stylish lady from Nortonville.

Dressed so fine, with matching jewelry on, I can see her still.

Everyone received a gift at Christmas. No one was left out.

Her choice of gifts was perfect, making everyone happy—no doubt!

She gave her all as a member in the ladies' club and worked with the best of them.

Helping neighbors and those in need was her passion. She would say, "OK, when?"

She came from Southern Illinois with a two-year old, traveling on a train.

Gritty and brave was she, venturing north to find work, and there she did remain.

In her older years, she suffered a stroke, but never lost her desire to give.

This was typical for Grandma; her strength and stamina were evident each day she lived.

She would join me in singing hymns, while rocking in her chair.

Her voice was shaky and a little off-key, but to me it was beautiful—none can compare.

Aunt Beulah Bell

Aunt Beulah, a more fair-minded lady we do not know.
Respect and love for you continue to grow.
Loyalty to your husband, James, your heart did revere.
Your giving spirit is so evident throughout each year.

In your Airstream camper, what travel you achieved!
With a career in nursing, a retirement you did receive.
Wednesday lunches with friends were dear to your heart.
Your years have outreached your family, who did depart.

Through health problems, with endurance, you passed every test.
Even though you had no children of your own, as "aunt" you are the best!
God has granted you many years to enjoy loved ones and friends.
Aunt Beulah, have a great 94th Birthday! Our love for you will never end.

AUNT HELEN CROW

Helen was quite a lady.
A better aunt, you'll never find!
--always cheerful and kind.

She and her beloved Gib were truly a
complete pair.
Their love and devotion spilled over—for
others to share.

"Ma Crow" was admired at Illinois
College's Camm House.
She was a loyal worker and a valuable
part of the team—there's no doubt!

Helen and her twin, Mary, loved to shop.
You would see them all around the town,
shopping till they dropped, or
enjoying every stop.

Mushrooms were one of her favorite
foods.
With her big sack, she would climb any
fence in the woods.

The "annual" fishing trip to
Hickory Hollow,
Missouri was something she would not
miss.
Did she fish? We're not sure, but visiting
with family filled her heart with bliss.

Coordinating the Crow Reunion was
definitely to her credit.
Without her efforts, where would the
family be?
We thank you, Aunt Helen, for all you've
done in your 81 years.
Our hearts say, "Farewell," but your love
and care we will always see!

"angels"

. . . . .watching over me. Thank
you, God, that your messengers are here.
Many times they comfort me when life seems
very cruel. Many times they attend to my
    needs when my heart is filled with fear.

Angels must have been there when we just
made it over a Florida canal bridge.
Angels were certainly around when Kirby
turned the tractor over on the pasture's
    ridge.

Angels were attending to Kyla when she fell
off the Harley that day in May.
Angels were watching over Kerry when he
inhaled the kerosene. My, how we prayed!

Angels directed the piece of the nail head so
Harvey had 20/20 vision and could see.
Angels have a busy schedule, watching over
    me!

AUNT MARJORIE

You are so brave; your courage is great.
You have lived away from home; you did not hesitate.

Yours songs at the Christmas parties delighted all your friends.
Your memory for all the words of the songs seemed to have no end.

Your sense of humor is delightful and refreshing. You always see
the good in everything that comes your way.
You really are a 'trooper!' What can anyone say?

When you received the accordion as a gift, the joy was on your face.
You started playing and singing. No one could ever take your place.

The doll you received for Christmas made you give an instant reply.
"Come here, girly," you said to the doll, with a twinkle in your eye.

When you get to Heaven, the Lord will say to you, "Come here, girly.
I have a special place prepared for you."
You will be happy. You'll be home with your loved ones, in your new
residence. Your joys will not be few.

Shield My Family, Oh Lord

We struggle in the relationships of life.
We fight against each other as in the last days.
Our families have met some of the wiles of the devil.
We should be looking above and singing your praise.
We should be lifting up our brothers, sisters, husband, wife, cousins.
We should love our family members with such a passion that nothing
can break through our commitments to each other.
Lord, put a shield of protection around our families.
Fill their days with happiness and fulfillment.
Guard them from danger.
Praise you, Jesus, for your saving power.
Thank you, Lord, for your grace and favor covering our family.

God Made Us a Family

There are no mistakes when God gives us life.
There is a purpose for each life He has given.
Each one of us is special. No one is better than the other.
Each of us has been given talents and characteristics by the grace of God.

A family loves one another, protects one another and never gives a false report.
No one needs to feel of lesser value as a person, based on anything material.
There is no place for jealousy, for all are special in their own way.

Our prayer is that each member of the family will love and respect all the other members.
Money, status, and possessions are gifts from God and do not make anyone above another.
God made us a family.

Erosion

The beating of the wind, rain and sun washes
   away the sand and changes the shoreline.
Spiritual decline, economic burdens, and moral
   and personal failures also chip away at the
   rock of our home and marriage.
Each time the tide of change and disappointment
   laps at our life, erosion can occur.
No matter how much the sand is removed from
   around our feet, we must stand firm.
"A house divided against itself will surely fall."

Bill and Lucille

Uncle Bill has been a farmer his entire married life.
He did a wonderful thing when he took Lucille as his wife.
They are the proud parents of three girls and one bouncing boy.
It's easy to see that their family fills their hearts with joy.

Aunt Lucille helped her father care for her two brothers.
She gained her experience in cooking delicious meals after the
    death of her Mother.
Lucille gave her continued support as a loving wife and mother
    while living in Missouri.
Today, Mason's Market is blessed because she makes the best
    potato salad and slaw—yes, siree.

Bill and Lucille have dedicated their lives to serving the Lord.
Memories of them coming down the aisle at Youngblood Church
    with their family in a line, are permanently stored.
I remember their kissing embrace in the kitchen long ago, which
    showed their love and care.
It made me realize this aunt and uncle had many more years of
    love to share.

Whether farming in Illinois or Missouri, Uncle Bill continued to
    till the soil.
In later years, he has added benches and pretty wooden pieces.
    With his carpentry, he does toil.

As a young couple, with small children, we were always welcome
    in their Missouri home.
Our trips to the Mexico, MO area were exciting and will forever be
    a happy memory for the Crows—because not too far from the
    nest could they roam.
"Be healthy; drink that milk. It's good for you," Uncle Bill would say.
He would tell funny stories at the table, or we'd go to the Ozarks with
    them—Oh, what happy days!

Bill & Lucille are dependable. With their love, they are truly free.
You can always count on them—whether it's canning corn, moving,
    helping with family illness/death, or sitting at the hospital during
    a surgery.
So, keep on singing those heart-warming solos, Uncle Bill. You are
    singing a song with your life every day.
Enjoy your dancing, be it line, round, or square. Congratulations on
    Your 50 years as man and wife. Thank you, and we love you.
    What more can we say?

Joe and Ruth Ella

There is a couple named Aunt Ruth Ella and Uncle Joe.
Through the years they have become very special to know.
Whenever we needed help, they were certainly there.
Whether moving, or at parents' deaths, they showed they cared.

To Homestead, FL, for a 'sunny' honeymoon, they did go.
But a Morgan County farm was calling—their love to sow.
Their children, Vernon, Mark and Lynn, we love—grandchildren, too.
Uncle Joe and Aunt Ruth Ella, we thank you. May God bless you.

Happy 60th Anniversary!
Harvey & Karen

Bonnie and Bill

How many years has it been since Bonnie met Bill?
It may be 50, but it seems only yesterday that they lived down on
   "Mockingbird Hill."
When Aunt Bonnie was dating Bill, I met this handsome young man.
He would walk me up his legs and turn me over with his hands.

This happy couple moved to Woodson on Vaniter Street.
Visiting Aunt Bonnie and Uncle Bill, eating fried potatoes, and riding
   my bicycle around town was very neat.

Then Orris' and the Crow's took a trip to Yogi Bear campground and the
   Opry at Petersburg, and on to Branson's Silver Dollar City.
You should have seen Uncle Bill going to the pool in his shorts and
   engineer boots! It was a sight to see!

Bonnie Lou has been a member of the Nortonville Club for years.
She cleans houses, cans, baby-sits, makes pillows and doll blankets.
   The quilt she made for me brought some tears.
She was a waitress, years ago, at the Woodson Sale Barn.
Today, she's still Aunt Bonnie—helping to freeze sweet corn.

Uncle Bill travels to Scottville to sort of a clubhouse.
One could hear what those men talk about in that special place—if
   only one was a mouse.
Deer and coyote hunting are sports Uncle Bill enjoys.
You could always see him sitting at Levi's Corner waiting on the boys.

Since the Crows' and the Orris' built homes about the same time, it was
   exciting and fun.
The Orris' helped us move (just as several times before) when our new
   home was done.

He visits Murrayville nearly every day for coffee with Uncle Joe in the
   office of the elevator.
Uncle Bill always said he had "this speed and one slower." In the fast
   pace of today, we'll see the other speed later.

Aunt Bonnie is dedicated to serving Youngblood Church and every
   function in Nortonville.
She performs her duties—you can count on her! You'll find her on
   Sunday morning sitting in the pew—without fail!

Happy 50th Anniversary!

Uncle Howard

Howard is a man of few words,
with a heart as big as all outdoors.
Riding his Harley Davidson Motorcycle
with his
sweetheart, Ruby, gives him great pleasure.
It's hard to believe he is 80 years old
because
the whole world he loves to explore.
What fun it is—going to the river for some
fish!
The rewards are beyond measure.

Family is important to Howard and they are
included on any ride, even to Sikeston, MO.
He'll even purchase special beds for those
who come to visit—sheets and all!
Dedication to his work at Kraft Foods gave
him
satisfaction until retirement, he decided to
go!
Howard, you're an example of growing old
gracefully.
In the eyes of your family, you stand tall.

A Teacup for

Friends

Mr. & Mrs. Graham

I've always thought of Mr. "G" as one of my truest friends.
Many times, I relayed my deepest thoughts and secrets to him; I knew
that's where it would end.
Every morning, when he arrived at work, I would be trimming away
on models and he would say,
"Hey, buddy!" Then I would say, "How are you?" He would always
reply, "Splendid." What a positive attitude to have each day!

No one could make a retainer or bend a wire as easy as Mr. "G."
But, who picked out his splinters from his hand? It was (artsie, fartsie) me!
Property lines became a problem, when Evens' farm wasn't Kirby's
Grandpa's, while quail hunting.
It was me who taught him to find coupons for diapers and food for
Grandbaby bunting!

After working with Mr. "G" for seven years, I got to know him quite well.
We have many common interests—woodworking, tools, the farm.
Oh, what stories we could tell!
I would say, "Kirby, Jr. "G" said . . .." I'd tell Mr. "G" "Kirby said. . . ."
What confidence I had in those two!
With two men of such fine reputations, wouldn't you?

Mr. "G" could fix anything—from running stools, flat tires, to building
shelves and sharpening dental tools. But, cleaning was not his forte'!
With the exception of his spoon (which he cleaned by stirring it in his coffee
cup), I cleaned the lab area and rearranged all his "treasured" photos while
he was away.
Mother Kay stopped by the office between her swimming and beauty
appointments each week.
For Mr. Graham's lunch, she would send fruit—instead of fattening foods—
--his good health to seek.

In her profession, Nurse Cloe, also Mother Kay, nurtured her family.
She made a nice blanket for Caulyn that became his security!

My family and I enjoyed our visit to the Graham's cabin in Matanzas Beach.
Mr. "G" always mentions how well Cloe could fish!
I admire you both for raising a successful family.
If only I could follow your secret remedy!

HAPPY 50TH ANNIVERSARY, Mr. & Mrs. "G!"

A Teacup and You

It doesn't take much in life to show a friend you care.
Just sit down together and secret treasures you can share.
Visiting with a friend is one of the sweetest things I know.
You can laugh or cry; your true feelings you can show.
It doesn't matter what time of day, morning, night or noon.
Just sit down with me; our hearts will be in tune.
I'll take some of your delicious bread and tea.
It will be more precious, when you sit down with me.
No matter how many miles separate us, it's perfectly OK.
Concern for each other, through a phone call, can brighten the day.
Tell me your heartaches and I'll tell you mine.
Our dear families are important to us. We give them our time.
We get weary in well doing, but a friend will always be there.
It doesn't take much in life to show a friend you care.

Friends of Mine

Friends of mine are varied in character. I have one of every kind.
Each one has their own strengths and weaknesses—like every human has.
If I can look at the strengths and ignore the weaknesses, I am blessed by each friend.
Even though I may not share these, I can appreciate their desires
and understand the differences in each friend.
Interests and experiences are varied in each one.
We all have environments and happenings that mold us into what we become.
If we have not walked in their shoes for a mile or two,
we cannot judge them for their actions or feelings.
Every contribution we make to life should be accepted
and seen as the best of the assets we possess.

Friendship

Friendship begins with love and trust and knowing that
someone cares.
A friend loveth at all times and keeps you in their prayers.
Even though you may act more friendly than everyone else,
a friend knows your faults and failures and loves you anyway.
When I'm worried and need someone to talk to,
I can call a friend and know they care about me.

Friends at ISVI

Friends, you mean so much to me.
So grateful to all of you, I will ever be.
Even though I have my faults, you accepted
me as I am.
You are the best of ISVI and helped carry me
through many a darn jam.
I will never forget you—for you can discern
the truth as it really is.
Life is not fair. It never will be. But boy,
can't we get ourselves in a fizz?
You are not blind, or visually impaired, but
you do see.
I love you all. You are special and will always
mean the world to me.

To My OMH Friends

As I end my state of Illinois
career, OMH, I want to thank
you.
You have welcomed me and
treated me like I would want
someone to do.

Your acceptance of me was a
great gift I'll always treasure.
My new friends at 319 East
Madison, Suite 3B, will be
memories beyond all
measure.

No matter what the problem,
no matter what the task, the
OMH will come through.
There is no doubt that when
the dust has settled, standing
there--will be you.

"Deer" Donald

Donald was coming out of the timber and said to H.C.,
"I don't know about this thing. I think we are getting
    too old to keep up with these young puppies.
    Deer hunting is slowing down, or could it be
    just H.C. an D.V.?"

"Our eyes are getting worse. Our hearing is going bad,"
    says Don, "but this hunting is some of the most
    fun we've ever had."

Without a deer this, there's no button on the hat and a
    sad song Donald will sing.
"Maybe we ought to hang our guns up and start carrying
    grenades se we can hit these darn things."

Now, you've got your wish, Don! Go out and have some
    fun!
Watch out, little deers, your lives are at stake. Donald's on
    the run!

VENA

A more loyal friend, or hard worker, you'll never find.
Mowing her large yard, having the cleanest garden,
  and sewing for friends—yes, she's the independent
  kind.

Her husband once said, "She works so slowly," and her
  mother-in-law replied, "Yes, but she works all the time."
Several winters spent in California helped make her life
  sublime.

Her love for the outdoors is true. Tending to her flowers
  and bushes, she can certainly do.
If you desire a good country meal, she can sure take care
  of that, too.

A fine Christian lady, a leader in God's work; she finishes
  each and every task.
Many young lives have been touched through her dedication
  to the Intermediate Class.

Her love and kindness was expressed caring for a special
  stepdaughter and her second husband—a dying man.
Thankfulness and appreciation are not enough to express—
  just try, if you can.

She loves to visit with neighbors and friends. She has many
  amusing stories to tell.
If you're wondering who this fine person is, it's my step
  grandmother, Vena, and she's swell!

Irene Whitman

When we think of Irene, it comes to mind how she labors in love.
Whatever she chooses to accomplish, it is blessed by God above.
Her work at Youngford Baptist Church is the love of her heart.
From VBS, to cleaning, to attending, Irene always does her part.

She and Raymond raised their children in the nurture and admonition of the Lord.
Louie, Herman, and Betty have a legacy that in their hearts will be forever stored.
Irene cans and freezes fruits and vegetables like you wouldn't believe.
With her heart fixed on the Lord, there is nothing she cannot achieve.

Happy 80th Birthday to a friend and neighbor

Getting all the Medals I Deserve

All men and women deserve credit for their labors,
their accomplishments, and their contributions
in life.

But, remember, life isn't fair. Sometimes,
recognition doesn't happen. Sometimes, there are
no awards.

Grandmother Vedder always said, "Give me my
roses while I am living."
So, if you have any good to say about a family
member, friend, or neighbor, say it now, so they can
hear it.

Precious medal is just that! Words of appreciation
are more valuable than silver or gold!

Here's to the Woman

Here's to the woman who knows where she is going
and won't stop until she gets there.
Here's to the woman who knows not only what she
wants from life, but what she has to offer in return.

Here's to the woman who expects no more from others
than she is willing to give.
Here's to the woman who meets life's challenges head
on and gracefully accepts both victories and
disappointments.

Here's to the woman who can be successful and
self-confident without losing her ability to be
understanding and compassionate.

Here's to a very special woman. Here's to YOU!

Dean and Jean

How good you look and what a special couple you are!
From farming in Murphysboro, but you didn't go too far.
The Highway Department and School District gained two who can pass any test.
Your nine grandchildren must know you are the very best.

God blessed you with five sons, who carry on your good name.
Remembering the great meals you prepared, they surely brought family fame.
May God bless you with many more years together, as you travel on life's way.
You are an example of hard work and love—what more can anyone say?

Morningside

Just as the sun will come up in the morning,
Morningside will rise and shine.
People will come from far and wide to see it's
beauty and feel its joy divine.
They will rest upon the peacefulness of the
streets and be filled with the Word of God.
Grace is the message received by those who
enter--wherever their feet may trod.
Praise God for his restorative power and His
love forever new.
Trust, Delight, and Commit. May His love
shine through you!

My Friend, Jane

There is a friend of mine I've had since childhood days.
Murrayville Grade School is the place we met so many
years ago.
The road of life has taken her to the mountaintop and
through some valleys.
She remains steadfast in her faith—the love of the Lord
to show.

Jane is a friend to all she meets—no matter the place or
time.
To this Christian lady, children in other towns deserve
Bible School, too.
She provided Godly fun in Ashland and Naples—with
joy sublime.
Leading someone to the Lord is what she desires to do.

Caring for the elderly is also a passion, not all work, for
Jane.
She gained love and respect from her co-workers, it's
true.
Her Winchester classmates are special and the
memories still remain.
LeaAnne, Paul and grandchildren know family ties are
many—not few.

Jane is content wherever she is, in whatever situation,
thankful she will be with her uplifting spirit, laughing
and talking to her is such a blessing for me.

RONNIE

When it comes to bosses, none can compare!
RGP has always been kind, considerate and fair.

The stress he bears is far to excess.
He presses on through budget, legislation and
    all the rest.

His Italian flair comes across once in a while.
Even so, he encourages us to get the job done—
    with style!

In times of grief, you can count on him to be
    there.
Distance—no problem! Finding the Crows' Nest—
    maybe; but he doesn't give up. He comes
    through—his love to share.

Thank you, Ronnie, for all you mean to our Division.
You will get your blessing in due season.

SANDY

Sandy is a kind lady who has her "head on straight."
Her smile is contagious, a great atmosphere to create.
She doesn't need Periwinkles--her own style to display.
Sandy possesses the gift of decorating her home and life each day.

Bonnie, Kim and Macy are blessings to Sandy, you see.
Two grandchildren add to the fun for this young-looking lady!
She loves traveling the world, seeing new sights, with family each year.
To Sandy the pilot, farm-owner, card-player, and loyal friend,
    let's give a cheer!

Happy 50th Birthday!

66

Risk Management

The management of risk centrally is a very complex
    task to do.
Rick is the manager of this endeavor. His controlling
    skill and executive ability have been proven—
    tried and true.

The chance of "injury, damage or loss" will inevitably
    prevail.
Do not fear. The careful, tactful treatment of the above
    three dangers by Ron, Don, Sam, Tom, Sue
    and the "rest of the crew" can manage any
    situation and direct activities very well.

Which single source do you have need of? Is it Workers'
    Compensation, Operations/Services or Auto Liability?
Each is equally distant from the center and accessible.
    Just contact the principle employee and you will see!

From any given point, on any given day, the employee in
    the appropriate Risk Management position can
    handle your problem in the most professional way!

HE STIRS
OUR NEST

Where is home?
"The way back home"

Haven't I been down this road before?
Why does this look so familiar?
Am I returning to do it correctly this time?
Is this a rerun or a second opportunity?

Thank you, Lord, for retracing my steps back to where I started.
Maybe I need to go back over my travels and experiences.
I will definitely consider alternate routes next time.

Which way is home?
Which fork of the road do I take? Right or left?
Will my home still be standing there?
Will someone welcome me with open arms?
Where is home? Is it only in my dreams?
Is it the home I would like to remember?
Is it destroyed or rebuilt?
Or is it just a memory of long ago?
If I find my home, will there be happiness again?
Will my presence make any difference?
Will friends and family want to visit this home?

If I could retrieve the valuable steps of my previous venture,
forget the mistaken avenues,
and use You to guide me along that Perfect Path,
I would surely be at the desired location.

After all, isn't home where the heart is?
Change my heart, Oh Lord!

He Stirs Our Nest

Yes, He stirs.
When life seems calm and safe, He gets our attention.
He ruffles our feathers. He shakes our nest.
We must look to Him for direction and safety.
The unstableness of our nest moves us to listen.
Whatever the rustling may cause, He has the answer.
We know He will not leave us or forsake us.
He goes through each situation with us.
As our nest becomes settled again, we are thankful.
Growth is the result of each stirring.
We appreciate the peace.

Hospitality

Welcome!
Make yourself at home.
Come on in and sit a spell.
Would you like something to eat?
Let me fix you some iced tea and cookies.
What more of a friendly world can I create,
If I treat my guests like I would like to be treated?
A stranger deserves to be treated in the same manner.
A generous, warm reception is what my guests deserve.
A friendly "How do you do?" is better than silver or gold.

Do unto others, as you would have them do unto you.

Life "down on the hill"

Life on the hill where I was born was so simple and sweet. It met all my needs. My marriage began there. Love was there. Peace was there. The grape harbor was there. Jelly was to be made. The wringer washing machine was there. Clothes needed to washed and rinsed in the galvanized tub. They loved to be hung on the clothesline to dry freshly in the sun and wind. The back porch was there. My two little boys loved to take their bath in the same wash tub, splashing water on the concrete floor. It was precious. However, running water was not there. It only ran when I ran to get it. Our drinking water was strategically placed at the bottom of the hill. What did that matter? The opportunity to walk down for a bucket was definitely there. Or, maybe taking the wagon and bucket—along with two little boys. Of course, some of the water was spilled before we reached the top of the hill. The cistern, or water for washing clothes and bodies, was at the back door. This was a real luxury. Just a few steps and there was water for cooking, doing dishes, and washing clothes. Oh, yes, the dirty wash water ran down the hill when it was poured out the back door.

Oh, if only I had kept that white enamel table with the red trim around the edges. I can remember the kitchen wallpaper with ironing boards, clothes hanging on the line and the words "Many hands make light work." It must have been special because even an old friend remembered those words and mentioned them many years later.

Where did all the peaceful feeling go? When did it leave? Did life get so complicated that there was no time to slow down and "smell the roses?" What a pity!

All the comforts of life are a welcome change. In our second home, the well and cistern were both at our back door. Having a bathtub and a kitchen sink in our third home was like moving right up town. Our daughter was born when we lived there. She was sad when we left the memories of her birth home for our fourth home, which we built out of brick. It provided a place for all the neighborhood kids to come to play, eat our bologna, ride our mini bikes, and our ponies. We were thankful for this new abode and welcomed all to come in through our doors.

Time goes on. Trouble may come. Disappointment may come, but the grace of God continues. Our fifth home was a singlewide mobile home. We were even back "down on the hill" but with all the conveniences of life this time. The water came into our home, conveniently, for all of our needs.

Now, in our sixth home, we are blessed to be living in a doublewide. It is warm and cool, yet practical and so lovely. It is a homestead nestled in the trees, which act as a windbreak. God is good! He is merciful and kind! I certainly hope that my next home will be a heavenly one. Whatever the Lord has in store for me will be His will and accepted as that. Praise His name! God is good all the time. All the time God is good!

"Looking Back"

I see hopes, dreams, fun times, family gatherings,
  few expectations.
I see a house with no modern conveniences, no
  running water (only down the hill).
I see my husband coming down the road on his tractor.
I see two little boys playing in the dirt, with two
  puppies by their sides.
I see Grandma and Grandpa sitting on the back porch,
  drinking iced tea.
I see two brothers admiring their new baby sister
  on the bed.
I see a home being built from the ground up.
I see a white German shepherd, riding on the enloader
  of the tractor.
I see an old Volkswagen with the fenders off. Is that
  mud all over it?
I see lots of neighbor boys at my kitchen counter,
  eating lunchmeat.
I see a daughter rearranging her room again.
I see many memories of the past.
I cannot see the future.
I *must* live for today.

On Stage

Each of us is "on stage" every day of our life.
We are actually performing whether we realize it or not.
The way we talk and walk is on exhibition daily.
If we say one thing and do another, someone will surely notice.
If we walk ungodly steps, it will be viewed by someone.
Being "on stage" requires practice—in whatever talent we possess.
A natural ability may be present, but it must be carefully
and continuously groomed for perfection, or near perfection.
Some performers may "take a fall," tumbling off the stage.
Healing the wounds and getting up are what is necessary at this point.
Sometimes the hurts of life are painful, but after the healing process,
the performance is stronger and ever more beautiful to watch.

What is an Inheritance?

An inheritance is not anything money can buy. It is not material. The best inheritance is one that leaves a legacy of beliefs, convictions, and morals. It is love, commitment, unselfishness, and examples of what is important to a great life. An inheritance might be just blessing your children and proclaiming that they are now a man, or now a woman. It entitles your offspring to grow up as men and women of God, knowing who they are in His sight. A parent's blessing gives their children the sweet spirit to be the man or woman of God He envisions them to be.

Anything in life that is worthy of praise is usually difficult to accomplish, yet worthy to cherish. Anything worth doing in life, whatever profession or goal, is sometimes very difficult to gain, but well worth the price to attain it.

Treasure your inheritance, not for what it can give you materially, but for the eternal value it possesses.

"Standing in the Gap"

When I was a child, "standing in the gap" meant,
   "Don't let the cows go through the gate or
   into the field. Head them off," said Dad.

As I grew, this term referred to helping Mother with
   housework, washing, yard work and gardening.

After my marriage, "gap-standing" related to getting meals
   for hired men, picking up boys to help bail hay,
   and running errands for equipment parts, etc., etc.

In my more mature years, my "standing" alludes to praying
   for God's watch and care over my family,
   baby-sitting with precious grandchildren and
   telling them how Our Creator made them so special
   and is "standing in the gap" every minute for them.

My place of "standing in the gap" changes as the years go by.
   May I be found "standing."

"to buy or not to buy"

It is a decision that must be made—an easy decision, it is not.
Having one's own home and property would produce a sense
    of well being.
Just remember, though, you must add taxes and upkeep to your
    list of expenses. You will have a payment for several
    years to come.
A "home" is where you hang your hat. It is where your heart is.
    It is a haven of rest from the storms of life—or should be!
A "home" should have a mat, welcoming others to its door.
    It should be a place of love and peace.
Problems will come and go, but they should not be allowed to
    interfere with the home's atmosphere for long.
Anywhere can feel like home when the Lord is there and
    peace abides.

Shape Up

Get your house in order.
Get your heart in order.
Get your priorities in order.
Get your body in order.
Shape up!

Clean those nooks and crannies of your
    home, body and emotions.
Exercise God's authority as His child:
    "a ...1, a...2, a...3....."

Throw out all the rubbish—unused in
    the past.
Throw out damaging thoughts, negative
    thoughts, and impure thoughts.
Keep only those valuable things that
    edify and lift up. These are lovely!

Come Let Us Reason

Reason

Come, let us reason.
We have been given the ability to
   think and choose.
   God made us above the animals.
Consider the options available to you
   and then draw conclusions, based
   on right thinking and the good
   sense God gave you.
As long as our motives are pure, we
   are justified in our reasoning.

What causes am I defending? Are
   they worldly or spiritual?
   Because of Him, everything
   in life is explainable. There is
   no need to argue.
God is not the author of confusion.
   We are of a sound mind and can
   reason.

Rights

We have the right to be heard; to
   be safe; to be informed; to
   choose freely; to remain silent;
   to representation; to be considered
   innocent until proven guilty; to
   say "No" to life, liberty and the
   pursuit of happiness.
These inalienable rights must be
   respected. They cannot be given
   away or taken away if we choose
   wisely.
If we do not obey the laws of God and
   man, some of our rights can be
   transferred to another owner.
God forbid, that we relinquish our
   precious rights in this way!

Peace

What is peace? (freedom from war, quiet, order, security,
    calm, reconciliation)
Peace is acceptance.
Peace is accepting a hospital admission instead of vacation.
Peace is rain on the roof of your mobile home.
Peace is rest.
Peace is letting go.
Peace is being a friend to oneself.
Peace is willingness to give up something for something else.
Peace is watching others fellowship while you are alone.

Peace of mind.
        Peace, be still!
                Oh, sweet peace.

"committed"

To what am I committed? To whom as I committed?
Am I committed to my job? my school?
As I committed to my husband, my family, my boss,
    my Lord?
Do I pledge myself to be true to my commitments?
Do I deliver the goods?
Am I someone a friend can truly confide in?
Am I worthy to entrust with their heartfelt thoughts
    and cares?
Where do I need to involve myself?
What do I need to let go of?
When will I honestly commend, or hand over for
    safekeeping, all my possessions of value in my
    life to the Lord?

Finalize

Isn't it time we finalized some things in our life?
Isn't it time to say those kind thoughts and do kind deeds?
Give the gifts we have one for another, including the treasures
   we have kept for our children.
Talk to that person we need to settle something with.
Don't put off till tomorrow, what we can do and say today.
Life is terminal (our physical body). We begin to die the
   minute we are born.
If we feel an urgency to do something today, we should do it.
   Life is short. However, God isn't finished with us yet.
   We are still on the merry-go-round of life.
Only what is done for Jesus will last.
At the end time of our life, we ponder the question, What
   have I accomplished? Did I meet my goals? Or God's
   plan for me?
Our goal is to be "at home" with him—with no more thereafter.
I have finished my course. I have fought the good fight.

"down in the valley"

You can see Jesus better in the valley.
On the mountain top he is more difficult
     to envision.
Looking to the Lord and keeping our eyes
     on the vision of where we are going,
     enables us to endure whatever comes
     our way—even while in the valleys
     of our life.
We can maintain our stand because of the
     joy He gives us.
We know our final destination, in spite of
     a few hills, sharp curves, falling rocks,
     or blinding fog, rain or snow.
We will finish our journey, even when the
     road is rough and steep.
We shall finish our course.

<u>Keeping the Faith</u>

Keeping the Faith is what we must do!
Whatever comes our way, with Him, we will make it through.
Our Hope is in Him; there is none other.
Charity we must show to each and every brother.

We are His hands and His feet in this life.
So let's extend our love to others in their strife.
They will know we are His by the kindness we share.
Praise His name and go tell others that we care.

Reverse Position

Our way of thinking and our set of
　　opinions may hinder our progress
　　toward our future well being.

To be in our proper place, we must
　　retain some strength and knowledge
　　for ourselves, in order to be ready
　　to serve.

There's a time to speak and a time to
　　be silent.

The time to be bold is in giving praise
　　to the Lord.
Hold back nothing. BE BOLD in the Lord!

Blessing

Are you a blessing to others? Do you intentionally bless them?
A smile, kind word, gift, or a fresh-baked pie—all are blessings.
Asking God to show favor to someone is a blessing to him/her.
Any kindness, whether verbal, physical or spiritual, blesses those
    we come in contact with.
"Best Wishes" is a wish for happiness or success to those we bestow
    it upon.
May I be a blessing to others. How I hope someone will see fit to
    bless me.

Timing is Everything

Without timing, nothing will evolve.
Everything we do is in God's timing, or out of His timing.
God made the earth and its inhabitants with perfect timing.
It is no accident that we are in the right place at the right time.
Even in playing basketball, jumping at the right time, timing is the key.
Your stature is not the important factor. It is when you jump.
When you drive to an appointment with an invalid parent and you find
    a parking place right in front of the door, that is God's timing.
Luck is not involved here. God's will is involved.

Spur

What can "spur" me on?
What prickly instrument will be used
    to urge me on?
At what "point" will I press forward?

A spur on the back will strongly urge
    me on.
A calcium deposit, touching crucial
    nerves will aid me in "getting
    the point."

When will I be willing to advise and
    warn others and myself earnestly?

Spirit

Face life with boldness and enthusiasm.
Real courage must be mustered up to apply vigor
    and zeal to each day.
Attack each task with cheerfulness and daring.
Let your personality and sparkle be evident as you
    bear your soul with real meaning and intent.
As you dash through each day, may your loyalty be
    seen, glued to each endeavor.
A large dose of bravery has to be added to the
    ingredients of life's spirit.
A lively spirit is essential to overcome adversity
    and maintain a vivacious outlook in the midst
    of the storms of life.
Being spirit-filled is of utmost importance!

"very little light"

There is little light in the world today.
Just a little light makes a great difference.
Jesus is the light! He makes light where
    there was darkness.
If we just let our "little light" shine, we can
    make a difference for Him.
Light exposes darkness, or sin. Sin cannot
    hide in the light of Jesus.
Let your light shine wherever you are. Do
    NOT hide it under a bushel basket. Do
    NOT let Satan blow it out! Shine all over
    your world—your family, neighborhood,
    friends, coworkers, classmates . . . . .
Just a little light brightens the woes of our
    world.
Just a little light directs wandering and searching
    souls to the true light, Jesus.

Faces

Faces are all around us along our
way each day.
Some are happy, some are sad, some
impel us to study them in a
special sort of way.
A face lined with age stirs up a
profound respect.
There is wisdom tucked inside each
wrinkle—each one having many
experiences to reflect.
Some faces glow with a special sort
of shine.
It's the love of Jesus flowing from
the heart of his children—every
single time!

Discontentment

Is this all there is? Has this thought ever entered
    your mind?
Life is repetitious and tends to become boring at
    times.
Our daily routines are repeated with each new day.
It's not a matter of being ungrateful for being alive
    or having the opportunity to repeat each day's
    method of doing things.
It's just that, as humans, we expect more. We may
    not really know what "more" consists of.
In one sense of the word, discontentment may urge
    us on to greater things. Some long-dreamed goal
    or desire may be achieved because of a restless
    spirit.
Our displeasure with the status quo may inspire us
    to reach out for ways to satisfy our yearnings.
We are to be "contented where we are," but to have
    ease of mind, we may be required to move to a
    higher or different level, and then again, "be
    contented where we are."
Without a little discontentment, we would never
    achieve our goals.
Regardless of our attainments, we will desire "more."
In this life, yes, this is all there is . . . .

"discipline"

Being under control in any situation is an indicator
of discipline.
To not allow anyone or any circumstance upset the
training of one's mind or character is true discipline.
Much prayer is necessary to maintain control under
adversity.
To keep quiet, instead of retaliating with verbal response
requires real control.
The order of one's life can be seen. It can be manipulated.
to control one's words and actions is essential to self-
discipline.
Obedience to the Word is the only reward in that
achievement.
No one can push your emotional "buttons" unless you
allow them to.
Silence can be the greatest accomplishment you can
experience. Silence is golden--you know!

True Colors

What are my true colors? What are your true
    colors? Are they red with courage, purple
    with royalty, black with fear and disdain?
Whatever our colors, they seem to emerge at
    times of failure, disappointment and
    interrupted dreams.
Will the real you, please stand up?
Maybe the you I thought I knew would be easier
    to confront.
Where is the honesty in any situation?
Why is it so difficult to find the supportive
    color? The appreciative color? The color
    of love and attention?

Then, in good times, colors are also evident.
It is easy to fly colors that are attractive when
    all the world seems to be your friend, with
    smiles of a warm, friendly yellow.
One can feel real "cool" blue when all traces
    of conflict are missing from our lives.
The "true" color is emitted by actions. Only
    God knows the "true colors of our heart"
    (motive/intent).

Education

Where did you get your education?
At a local college or community
college, at a state school, at the
local high school, at the school-
of-hard-knocks, at a one-room
school through eight grades, or
out behind the barn?
Every skill, ability and experience
contributes to our education.
Knowledge is acquired from many
sources.
Wisdom is knowing how to apply
the knowledge we gain.
A degree from the most prestigious
university does not guarantee
wisdom.
Those who realize they do not have
all knowledge are the wisest.

"The tongue burning"

There is power in the tongue. It rules the body.
What proceeds from the mouth comes from the heart.
Why a burning tongue?
Is it yearning to speak for the Lord?
Should it be more willing to speak peace and knowledge?
Why a burning tongue?
Is it because of unkind words spoken?
Is it the result of unconfessed sin?
Lord, tame my tongue in the way you see fit.
Show me when my words are barren and dry.
Let me see the glory your words can bring.
Reveal to me words that can lift and not tear down.
Give me words that glorify your honor and power.
There is power in the words of my tongue.

Build a bridge and get over it

A bridge is built in order to go to the other side.
To the other side of what?
Could it be to the other side of a relationship, a marriage, a divorce?
A covering to go through to the other side is a welcome safe place.
This covering will protect us, along with the bridge, from the elements of life.
It can be a beautiful shelter while traveling from one rough road to another.
That rough road may be a health issue or a financial hardship.
Going through in spite of trials is what we must do.
Sometimes we turn a corner and there appears another bridge we must cross.
Never stop your journey. Build your bridge. Get over it and survive.

Hinges

What is at the gate of your heart?
What opens the door of fruitfulness in your life?
Without hinging your life on Jesus,
you will not see the vision beyond the door.
Without opening the door, the opportunities
beyond it will never be within your grasp.
When God closes a door, a new hinge will cause
another blessed door to open for you.

The gate of your life is available, if you will only g
through it.
The lid you remove will offer blessings you canno
contain.
Swing open your heart to gather in all the Word.

Cover my door with the blood of Jesus.
Equip me to work for you.
Hang my being on the door of Jesus.
Will you open the life gate and go through it?

Keeping the Peace

Have you ever tried to keep the peace?
  It's so difficult to do!
When sister and friend come to visit, and
  you have divorced parents, you might
  as well say, "That's it, I'm through."

Sister and friend desire to ride father's
  motorcycles.
Father is upset because sister is staying
  at mother's.
You invite sister, friend, father and family
  for a meal.
Mother suggests all go for pizza and puts a
  damper on the spirit for all the others.

Oldest son asks to ride along to take sister
  and friend to the airport. He asks his
  brother to go along, too.
Father is upset because he thought he'd be
  asked (by daughter) to go.
Yes, Mother wanted to go, but wasn't asked.
How about father and mother going together?
  Oh, no, that would never do!!

What is the solution to this problem?
  Tell mother and father to grow up and
  accept this situation, the way the family
  has had to do.
If they can't or won't, then say, "OK, dear
  parents, I've tried and tried and now it's
  up to you."

Wishing for Friday

The workweek has been long.
The weekend is coming, but when will I see
it?
Each Friday only makes my journey two
days closer to Monday.
But then, without Monday, how would I
ever reach Friday?
I realize that I am wishing my life away,
hoping the days will pass into another
weekend.
Then, those two days speed by so quickly.
There is not enough time to work, play, and
rest.
I must remind myself that each day I can
work means I am alive and healthy enough
to work.
I must enjoy each day for I may not have
tomorrow.

Life's Fragrances

Life's Fragrances

What aroma does my life portray?

There are many varieties or aromas—grandma's
 fresh-baked bread, the farmer's newly-plowed
 field and newly-mown hay, and the neighbor's
 freshly cut grass.
These smells are sweet and can clear our lungs with
 each grateful breath.

Perfumes and after shaves cannot compare to these
 natural fragrances.

Our life reflects fragrances of sacrifice, service and
 commitment.

The daily habit of prayer sends an aroma from our
 lives that will bless those we petition for—in
 ways only God can comprehend.

What is life?

Life is worth living.
Life is what we make it.
Life is just a bowl of cherries.
Life is so uncertain.
Life is not fair.
Life is good.
Life has its ups and downs.
Life is for the living.
Life is a gift.
Life is life.
Life is better than being six feet under the sod.

My Place

What is my place in life?
What is the space I must fill?
Many people fill up space in life.
The question is "Where is that perfect space?"
Sometimes just being there is all that is needed.
Sometimes saying the right words is what is important.
Sometimes taking action is what is required of us.
May I be in the right space at the right time.
May I say the things that are needed at that moment.
May I do the things that make a difference for someone.
Life is very fragile.
Life is but a vapor.
Life is like a fleeting moment in time.
Life will soon be complete.
When my life is at completion, my space is deleted.
When my life is completed, there is no more work to do.
When my life is ended, may the fact that I was living make a difference?

"smoke screen"

God can see through our smoke screens.
They may keep us separated from others—
    even protected. However, we cannot
    hide from God. He can penetrate any
    concealer we may camouflage.

His Word is the only shield we need.
    It is our defender, which the world
    cannot pierce.

We are but a vapor. Just as a puff of steam
    or gas evaporates, we will some day
    be separated from loved ones and
    acquaintances that we should NOW
    tell of God's love. We will rise just
    as particles of carbon rise as smoke.

Oh, Lord, may we tell our loved ones the
    truth, which will set them FREE.

Let us leave heavenly treasures here on
    earth, which cannot be destroyed.
    Such treasures will endure for eternity
    in the hearts of our family and friends!

Camping

Life is one continuous camping adventure.
It's not forming a temporary residence, with a
very simple shelter.
It's not setting up a tent by a stream or woods.
It's not even a military establishment, which
endures for a few years.
It's not just spending the night outdoors, without
comforts for a short time.
It is the people you choose in your "camp"—
family, friends, comrades.
The camp is the people living therein.
With whom do you want to camp with for the rest
of your life?
With whom do you want to roast weiners with, zip
your tent with, pour water on the fire with?
The campers and the spot are your choice and
your experience.

The Mystery of Life

Life is such a mystery. We don't always know our way.

We live trusting in the Lord to help us through each day.

We could go this way, or that; we're always looking for an open door.

When the door closes, He has something else for us to explore.

If we believe in Him, we know He has a plan.

Through each trial and struggle, with His help we will stand.

Our purpose is to tell others of His love for us.

We know the end, but it's for the journey that we must trust.

What is a purposeful life?

If my living has a desired goal and the
intention of my heart is honorable,
I am striving toward my purpose.
Even though I may not feel that I have
attained all the desires of my heart,
if I have been true to my family, including
parents, siblings, husband and children,
then my life has had a purpose and meaning.
Even though I have not achieved all my
goals in life, if I have worked an honest
day's work and been loyal to my supervisors
and to God,
I have had a purpose for which I can be
thankful to say is mine.
My co-workers should be able to see my
faith and receive some of the knowledge
of the goodness of my Lord and Savior.
Even though I may feel that I am not
appreciated by my family
or given a hug when I needed it, if I have
told them of my trust in the Lord,
and shown fairness to each of them, I have
given what is expected of a servant.

Hanging On

Hang on just a little bit longer. Whatever is happening in your life
   will only last for a season.
Anything in life that is worth having is worth waiting patiently for.
Thanking God for the trials and uncertainties is so important
   in our prayer life.
Hanging on could be just to keep on praying for a loved one in
   need, for protection, or for guidance.
Hanging onto our dreams is so important for our future.
Without a dream, our goal for life is impossible to approach
   with any great expectations.
Hanging on in the midst of heartache and pain is difficult.
Thanking God for the pain and suffering will reduce its intensity.
It is hanging on when no one seems to care is painful.
But Almighty God knows our heartaches and he cares.

Life is like a rainbow.

Many or all of the colors of the spectrum touch our lives.
Red stands for courage, bravery, and the blood of Jesus.
Yellow denotes laughter, warm feelings, or a baby's room.
Blues are fair skies, everlasting love, or a depressing Monday.
Green might be inexperience, or a thumb, or jealousy and envy.
Purple has power, majesty and dignity in its hues.
White says purity and peace, as in "wave the white flag."
Black can be despair, distinguished, or death tones.
Colors touch our lives every day—in a negative or positive way.
Fashion is important. Using the best colors for us is the key.
Our everyday language is strewn with the colors of the rainbow.
God, the most brilliant designer, uses the seasons as the key.
When you think your life is boring, just think of the beauty in it.
Remember how beautiful the sunrise or sunset sweeps the sky.
Just gaze at the mountain shadows and see their majesty.
Paint your life with colors of contentment, love and thankfulness.
Life is like the rainbow, coloring our world!

Undecided

When life offers all its choices, a
decision must be made.
Whether choosing right or wrong,
we live with our first thought.
No matter what the outcome, we
call a spade a spade. (a decision
was made)
After our choice is spoken, no
change can be bought.
Life can throw us some curves.
Some rough places may be found.
The curves can really get on our
nerves.
For the road of life, we are bound.
Learning to live with what we
choose can be very unnerving.
Waiting for the right moment to
move teaches us patience.
Even though we knew the right,
the outcome could be one that we
are deserving.

All our attempts to change the
facts won't matter to our closest
agents.
Right or wrong, which will it be?
It's your choice; don't you see?

Test of Courage

This is a test . . . . . (2-minute horn).
Life is a test.
One must muster up lots of courage to endure the
    trials of life.
It takes courage to stand by while your child is
    hurting.
It takes courage to walk away from a home you built.
It takes courage to face disappointment and crushed
    dreams.
It takes courage to hold your head high, change
    direction, and believe in a greater future.
ONLY GOD GIVES THAT COURAGE!!!

Sustaining Elements of the Feather
as it falls from
The Nest.....

Prayer
Commitment

Courtesy   Discernment
                      Concern
Love   Positivity
                         Support
Touching   Eye Contact
   Respect   Caring
   Attentiveness
                              Time
         Listening

                         Going....
      Consideration   Doing....
                              Being!

         Seeing
         Upholding

                    OTHERS

Wrap It Up

Send It Back

"crazy like a fox"

We should be eager to serve God.
He is worthy of our service, time and talents.
To serve with enthusiasm is even better!
We need to be crafty, like the fox, to find
    time and ways to be with the Lord.
We must be quick to do His work.
Our protection may well be a foxhole.
We may need to dodge into our hole
    (quiet place) to prioritize our life's
    work, duties and obligations.

"a fool for Christ"

If I'm not Christ's fool, then whose fool am I?
If I am acting foolishly, then why not act a fool
    for Jesus?
Why not have fun in the name of the Lord?
It is OK to play and to laugh at ourselves.
    Laughter is great medicine. It reduces stress
    tremendously.
Learning of Jesus' love for us from a clown or one
    showing love and concern to others is a way of
    seeing Christ's love.
We need to be vulnerable for Christ. We must
    be open to attack. We must be His fool. As
    we are victorious, His glory is revealed.

115

"wrap it up and send it back"

Have you ever wanted to wrap up something you were given in life and "send it back?"
The wrapped package could be pain received from a parent during divorce.
This package could be disappointment experienced from a friend's actions.
It could a package of being ignored by the one dearest to your heart.

Never the less, some packages just cannot be returned.
We must deal with it, learn from it, and continue on with our life.

Only God knows about all our packages, which we would like to return to sender.
Only He can turn the "hurtful contents" into something beautiful.
Only He can make the ugliness turn into a healing instrument.
The wrapping can become a soothing covering.

After all, it's what is in the heart of the gift that really counts.
The outer covering doesn't always reflect what is inside.
In wrapping it up and sending it back, we would miss all the lessons and growing
as a result of the package.

"in a garbage heap"

Sit still, daughter, so that I may dump my garbage on you.
Let me cover you with my past hurts, my improper decisions,
and my parents' wrongdoing!
If you will, allow me to tell you what's been on my mind for
many a moon.
Just bend over, cover your head, and welcome all the tin cans
of painful memories and the empty plastic bags of emotional
dung that I have endured.
Thank you, dear daughter, for your willingness to be my
garbage heap!

Personal Attachments

What do I find myself attached to? What am I fastened to?
    What do I have a bond arising with?
Are my personal attachments so valuable that I would be lost
    if they were not attached?
Do I prefer worldly possessions or those that will last?
Are my attachments those of family, neighbors, friends and
    those I come in contact with?
Do I give values, love and heavenly instruction, or negative
    and carnal thoughts?
May I attach myself to the will of the One who made me—with
    His plan for my life foremost in my thoughts.

Are You Listening?

Are you really listening to me? Do you hear what I am
    trying to convey to you?
Please, dear friend, listen and look past my new dress or
    my new haircut.
By the tone of my voice, you must know what is on my
    heart.
My smile is only to cover the hurt and confusion inside.

Are you really listening to me? Please, husband, don't
    consider my requests as nagging.
    Can't you tell that I just need your love and attention?

Are you really listening to me? Please, loved one, you
    must realize that I am human, too. I enjoy being here
    for you. Your appreciation is all I require. Are you
    listening?

117

"appreciate the value of a man"

Of what value is a man? a woman? a boy? a girl?
We are not of the value we think we are.
We are of the value we think others think that we are.
Examine your own value.
We are all special.
      We are all unique and made in God's image.
He is no respector of persons. Therefore, everyone
      has value.
Many do not know or feel they are of value.
Each has something to offer in life.
We are born for a purpose. It is to love,
      honor, respect and thank God for His
      mercy and many gifts to us. Some of
      those gifts are our talents, our ability
      to learn, to love, to worship him. The
      very breath we take from second to
      second is His gift to us.
When we appreciate man's value, we also appreciate
      God and His grace to us.

Why Shop?

Why are you always bringing a sack home with you, dear?
You have a problem.

Yes, husband dear, the problem is you never bring anything
home in a sack—unless it is tobacco or something to eat.

What about toothpaste, underwear, envelops, safety pins,
writing pens? What about your tie from the cleaners? What
about the gift for your niece's wedding, her baby shower?
What about the birthday and Christmas gifts for your very
children, dear? Don't forget those precious grandchildren.
What about the suspenders for long-waisted, heavy-set men
like yourself? You know the suspenders have to be the kind
that grab the pants firmly.

What is that you are hiding in that sack, dear?

Oh, do you mean this pair of shoes I purchased at Salvation
Army? Or, could it be the cat food? It just might be this sale
item from a rack at JC Penney, or a value deal from K-Mart,
found on any day. Or, the little sack you see could be my
blood pressure medicine, which I need because of the stress
upon me from all of this shopping and then listening to your
complaints.

If you are fortunate, you might find your favorite hot
peppers in this treasure sack from K-Mart. You might
locate a can of Spanish peanuts in this bag from Dollar
General.

Why should I shop at all? I believe it is time to appoint you,
hubby dear, to take this load off my shoulders. It's not a
heavy burden to add these purchases to your Coke and
various meats, is it? You're right, darling, why shop?

Second-hand Rose

"Second-hand Rose" does not always refer to clothes.
Take it from someone who certainly knows.

Parents don't care if you are fair.
Even when it's difficult—your love to share!

Children don't care, unless there's a favor you can do.
Otherwise, they just don't have the time for you.

Husbands don't care.
They think their wives will always be there.
Job, union, kids and friends—all are more important
than "Second-hand Rose."

Take it from a "Rose" who knows!

Storms Come
and
Storms Go

Serenity in the Calamity of the Storm

Even though the storm rages, He can give peace.
Our problems are easy when given to Him.
The storms of our life, He can calm.
When our calamities seem so large, call on Him.
He can correct any unclear situation.
Give it to Him for He is able to handle it.
Our attempts to solve strife will fail.
He cannot fail. Call upon His name.

Roll Back the Clouds

I want to see life clearly again, so roll back the clouds.
Roll back the hurt; roll back the rejection.
Roll back the bitterness and pain.

I want to see a reason to live again.
I want to cross over to the better side of life.

When I feel depressed, when I feel frustrated,
And when I feel hurt, roll back the clouds.
When I feel misunderstood, roll back the clouds.

When I am blamed unfairly, roll back the clouds.
When I feel sad and lonely, roll back the clouds.

Let the sunshine through the clouds around me.
Make my gloomy days sunny again.
Take away the rainy days of my life.
When life seems dreary with despair,
Make the sun beam its warm, bright rays on me.

May the dark gray areas of my life drift away,
Like the wind blows the clouds.
Change my outlook to beautiful rays of light and color.
May I feel light, fluffy and carefree, drifting on a
Cotton-like cloud of happiness.

121

Where Did the Joy Go?

Where are the happy days that were so sweet and dear?
Where are the smiles of yesteryear?
Why did the joy leave us? Where did it go?
Why did those years our caring not entrust?
Were we so unthankful of what we had back then?
Will we appreciate and cherish our treasures? But when?
What should our approach be? What should our actions show?
Would it possibly be that pure love is what we should accept and know.

"The wind at my back"

Even though I have struggles in my life, I know the wind is at my back.
Even though I am rejected, I know someone is pushing me on.
Even though my loved ones misunderstand me, I know I am loved.
Even though my work is unappreciated, I do it as unto the Lord.
You are the wind at my back.
You are my rock to stand on.
You are the peace I cannot otherwise find.
You are my strength for each task.
Storms may come, storms may go, but my faith is in You.
Storms may cloud my mind, my dreams, and my vision.
Storms may cause me to doubt my direction in life.
Storms may be the very answer to my prayers.
When trouble comes, my hope is in You.
When I feel defeated, I know I am a winner through You.
When all the things I hold dear are somehow shaken, You are there.
When life seems difficult, I can hold my head high, trusting in You.
You are the wind at my back.

The Hurricane

What is your hurricane in life?

Hurricanes destroy lives and businesses.
Hurricanes destroy property and shorelines.
What about the hurricane that breaks a heart?
It can never be mended.
You can purchase new furniture and a home to dwell in.
You cannot purchase a heart that is not scarred by disrespect and denial.
One can be safe in a home with a secure, storm-free protection.
One can be trapped in a place of pain and turmoil.
Only God provides a safe haven for the soul.

"the storms of life"

Sometimes we cry out for help.
Sometimes we do not.

He is always there in the midst of our
storms.

When the winds are blowing and the storm
is raging, He is our shelter.
He alone can calm the storm.
He can keep our vessel from going
or from capsizing.

The waves may be high; they may be strong,
but JESUS is STRONGER.

He will say, "PEACE, BE STILL."

Still Waters

Still waters run deep.
Some of our experiences in life are like gentle streams.
Some are like raging waves on the ocean.
No matter what shape the water may form, it is still the same.
Whenever its gentleness laps against our legs, it is soothing.
When the waves rise up and toss our ship, it can be devastating.
After the storm, the calmness is so much more appreciated.
The pitter pat of rain is a peaceful sound.
A sense of warmth and security is felt.
When the storms come, our well being is unsure.
We are not certain what the outcome will be.
Whatever storm comes our way, when we are rooted deep
in our commitments, we stand firm.
Still waters run deep.

Music is a Lighthouse

Just as the lighthouse directs its light from the shore,
so does music light the way to the soul.
Music can turn darkness to light. It can change a frown to a smile.
Music will turn anger into joy.
It can cause memories to ponder happy days gone by.
Music, in any beat or tune, causes the rhythm in one's body to move into action.
It changes night into day and war into peace.
The music of any culture is an open door into the hearts of its citizens,
with a language that touches everyone.
Music is a lighthouse.

125

Riding Around in a Whirlybird

Come down from out of the blue.
Come down from that "whirling bird in the sky."
Are you always going round and round in such a manner?
Do you ever touch earth and feel the security of the dirt under your feet?

Some of us are spinning around, going this way and that,
shifted by the wind—to and fro.
We cannot be suspended forever, above the hustle and
bustle of life below.

Hanging in the sky this way must be difficult, unless we are attached
to something above.

Let's refrain from our dizzy, confused condition.
Let's stop awhile.
Let's set our feet on something solid—Jesus, the Solid Rock.

Overboard

Have you ever fallen overboard?
Have you ever gone overboard?
When the storms of life come—and they will—we sometimes
get over-balanced and fall into the sea.
The water is dark and deep. We come up for breath.
Without a lifesaver, we fall into the depths, again and again.
We grope for a way to survive—a raft, board, inner tube, or a ship
to save us, which is really a hand from heaven, sparing us from
certain death.
Sometimes we indulge in extremes of enthusiasm.
Such an extreme could be overeating, credit-card shopping,
anxiousness, fearfulness and more.
We stand on our excuses for falling 'aside" of the plan for our life.
Any reason we fall "to the side" can be corrected with discipline,
perseverance and faith.
May we look above for assistance with our
overboard ways (tendencies).

Whirlwind Game

"Where's that whirlwind game?" said husband in a dream.
   "I don't have one," replied his wife.

But maybe they really do have a whirlwind game.

Life is a game played in a whirlwind. In the midst of the
   windstorm, we attempt to stay on our feet, while
   the storm is whirling us round and round.
At times, the wind is so violent, we feel like it could throw
   us to the ground—never to rise up again.

Our mind and emotions are whirling, too:
   Should we go this way or that way?
   Should we attempt this new venture?
   Should we be bold in the Lord or give our
      cloaks also?
   Where should we work? Where should we live?

On a game board, choices are not so permanent.
   Only God knows the game plan for our lives.
   He makes the jumps, the advances and the stops.

Thank you, Lord, that YOU are in control of all our
   "whirlwinds."

Winds of Change

I feel the winds of change blowing—all around me.
Who can tell what they may be?
Are they winds of uncertainty, winds of understanding?
Could they be changes of employment and residence?
Come, welcome changes.

The winds must blow. Otherwise, no changes could be seen.
The dried leaves and dead bark of our lives must be rearranged.
Hopefully, the unneeded and unwanted parts will be carried away.
Some winds are cold gusts and some are warm, gentle breezes.
Whatever gale, they will come.

Thank you, winds of change, that I may not lie dormant during
the winter of my life.
Stir me. Lift me. Place me in the proper place.
Lift my spirits and make me light of heart.
May I recognize others in the midst of their winds,
to catch them when they fall.

Thank you, winds of change.
You awaken me from my sleep of contentment.
May I not be so difficult to move that I cannot be
taken to a higher ground.

Come, Winds of Change!

Moving On......

"moving on"

Life is a series of "moves." Many changes occur before and
after these moves.

Each move prepares us for the next move we make. Likewise,
the moves in our past offer much-needed experience.

"Move your feet; lose your seat" applies here. Once we leave
a home, place of employment, or church home, our position
is altered—never to be the same. Even upon a return to that
place, all becomes new.

What more evidence is required to prove how important each
day is, as we live it—never able to retrieve one minute of
our days?

"Moving on" is a phrase truck drivers use. "Moving on down the
line" is exactly how we move through life. We will witness
steep mountains, small hills, long valleys, curves, bad
weather, obstacles in the road and detours. Patience is
imperative in order to deliver our load.

What glory is waiting when we come over a mountain, viewing
sunshine on a peaceful valley.

"a time to dance"

To dance in the Lord is a blessing unto God.
It is a form of praise to our Maker, the Giver of life
and breath, the Giver of all good gifts.
Our heart dances, and so should our feet praise Him.
We cannot contain our innermost joy in a motionless
state.
Our Maker put the whole world into motion and
everything therein.
Nothing stands still—not even time!
The ocean waves praise Him. The wheat in the field
praises Him. The trees move in their beauty.
Let everything that hath breath praise the Lord!

Downhill Slide

Have you ever felt like you were on a downhill slide,
rather than on an uphill grade?
Only after the grind of uphill experiences, can we
enjoy the smooth slide downhill.
Once we are at the bottom, or on level ground for a
period of time, it is certain there will be other
grades to climb (with varying percentages).
After having been in the valley, we can understand
the joy of being on the mountaintop.

132

"able to face anything"

"If I ever get through this situation, I'll
    be able to face anything." This statement
    is repeated oftentimes.
We never know what is around the corner,
    lurking in the dark.

Whatever trial it may be, we must not be afraid
    or anxious. We will not be given more than
    we can bear. It may be a new problem, or a
    recurrence of an old one.

Nothing is impossible with God. The initial blow
    is usually the worst. It is sometimes a shock.
    It may not shock you at all. It is never
    unbelievable. In any event, the emotional
    hurts can only be mended by the Lord.

We must keep our armor on, because we never
    know when the fiery darts may come, or
    where they may originate from.

Direction

Where should I work? What is my calling?
Am I in the right place? Tell me, Lord.
Which way should I go? Show me the way to go.
I have no compass but you. You are my light in the dark.
You comfort me when the winds blow and the waves get
high.
The storms may come but you calm my storms.
You are the master of the wind. You control my ship.
I know I am in good hands with you at the controls.
Have your way with my life. Steer me in the right direction
on life's troubled sea.

"line up"

We must take a position in life—many times.
Our rank and file is assessed by the choices of which line
    we choose to form.
Since a straight line is the shortest distance between two
    points, our position can result in a detour, or the quickest
    route to our destination.
Even our vocation denotes a "line of work." We have
    aligned ourselves in particular channels.

Get in Line

Is there something you wish to receive?
Is it free government cheese?
A ticket to a concert?
Cash from your savings account?

You must get in line!

Do you desire salvation?
Pardon for your sins?
It is a free gift.
Come before the Lord—get in His line.
Get on His team.

We must line up to His standards.
We must walk the straight and narrow way.
We must conform to the Will of God.

This Inner Circle

With what am I surrounded? In what orbit do I find myself
    traveling in?
Does my life revolve around earthly pleasures?
What group of people am I encircled by?
Is every point on my circle of life equally distant from the
    center—Jesus Christ?
What is inside my heart and soul, in the more private parts?
What are my secret desires? Are my innermost thoughts those
    which glorify God?
Will my family circle be unbroken?
Am I doing my utmost (through the welcome presence of the
    Holy Spirit) to secure my family circle?

The Last Mile

When is the last mile? How do we know when we have
traveled it?
Unless we are very ill, we cannot prepare for our last
minutes on this earth.
We must live each day as if it were our last mile and live it
to the fullest.
Any good that we can do, we must do before it is too late.
The last mile is also a very nice feeling when you have
been on the road for a week in a semi.
It means your family is just a mile away.
When one is weary and tired, sometimes the last mile
doesn't seem so bad.
Eternal rest could be a welcome sight to a weary traveler.

Marching Band

Have you ever felt the urge to go marching down the
street?
To hear the drum cadence while stepping to the beat?
Then why not practice diligently in the early morning
dew?
Get in line, do an about-face, watch the drum major's
baton and
listen to Mr. Well's instruction for you.
The half-time performance is something you won't want
to miss.
The precision of the marchers will fill your heart with
bliss.
Oh, yes, don't forget the pride you feel while
representing your school.
The fun you will have on band trips makes all the
practice a mere tool.

Leading the Way

Once we took a vacation with four other families.
My husband was the car in front,
"leading the way."

We can lead in many ways.
We don't have to be first to lead.
Our conversation, prayers, ideas, vision—all can lead
the way to someone's freedom.

One can be the least in the midst of many and lead
the way spiritually.

138

FROM PAIN

TO POWER

Have you ever had a heartache?

If you never had a heartache, how would you know that He could heal it?
If you never had a problem, how would you know that He could solve it?
If you never prayed for anything specifically, how would you know if you received it?

Every heartache healed is just one step further to maturity.
Every problem solved gives us the faith to continue searching for truth.
Every specific prayer answered confirms our trust in the Almighty God.

God can heal our heartaches, solve our problems, and answer our specific prayers.
And He does. With Him, life is worth the living and victories are won.

From Pain to Power

It's when we suffer with some form of pain
that we can acquire power.
This power is going through the pain
to the other side, victorious.

Your pain can either make you hungry
for something else or it will eat you alive.
Pain and disappointment will make you
bitter or better.

When we are weak, He makes us strong.
It is then that His power can be felt and seen.

HAVING PAIN

Having pain can work a miracle in your life.
It can draw you closer to the Lord.
Your dependence is wholly on Him.
Everything lasts only for a season.
When the time comes, it changes.
Pain can be an answer to prayer.
It can cause complete trust in Him.
Without pain, we are free to serve.
With pain, we can be served.
When God lifts the pain, what joy!
The joy of the Lord is our strength.
Praise God for his mercies.
They are from everlasting to everlasting.

A BROKEN WING

A certain crow fell from her nest and broke her right wing.
It shattered the wing and her plans, but in her heart she could still sing.
If rest was what she needed, from her busy life,
Rest she received, with some pain, and consideration for any strife.
Knowing her life was saved is witness that He's Lord of all.
It takes heaven's angels to catch us or to cushion our fall.

THE FALL

HAVE YOU EVER FALLEN AND DIDN'T KNOW WHY?
YOU MAY HAVE FALLEN FROM A RELATIONSHIP.
COULD IT BE THAT SOME BAD HABITS FELL OFF?
THE FALL MAY HAVE OCCURRED TO PRODUCE
CHANGE.
SOME NEW PRINCIPLES MAY FALL IN PLACE.
LOVE MAY BE REVIVED IN THE PROCESS.
FALLING IN LOVE WITH GOD'S MERCY AND GRACE
COULD BE THE RESULT.
TRIPPING THROUGH LIFE IS EASY, BUT
RECOGNIZING TRUTH IS DELIBERATE.
STEPS MEASURED BY DISCIPLINE WILL BE SAFE
AND FRUITFUL.
MAY MY FUTURE BE FILLED WITH HOPE.
MAY EACH STEP I TAKE BE GUIDED BY A STEADY
HAND.
MAY HIS PLAN FALL INTO PLACE AS I CONTINUE
MY JOURNEY.

HONORING
WARRIORS

"the dead deserve more"

*Memorial Day comes once a year. Shouldn't we honor
the dead every day?*
*Our forefathers—uncles, brothers, fathers, grandfathers,
daughters, as veterans, have helped preserve our freedom.*
Much sacrifice has been offered in our behalf.
*What about our grandparents, parents, friends, and neighbors
who have influenced our lives tremendously? Don't
they deserve honor, too? This honor is not just visiting
the grave site alone, but thanking God that He allowed
them to be a part of our lives. That He allowed them to
cross our paths.*
*If the dead deserve honor, then how much more we should
honor the living every day.*
*Each contact we make, each heart we lift, and each uplifting
word shows our support of them and our love of God for
his divine intervention in our lives.*

"wall of protection"

Does building a wall to protect oneself ensure safety?
Withdrawing, thus hiding feelings, emotions, and desires
from the entire world, is no guarantee of protection.
Throwing oneself into one's work will result in
suppression and eventually frustration.
To prevent contact with friends is isolation and abuse
to self.
Only when one tears down the wall he has been hiding
behind, can true living begin.
Exposing oneself to the world and others makes us
vulnerable.
How can one be a conqueror if he is not open to
attack?
Faith in God is our only "hedge of protection."
May I be bold in serving, knowing He watches over
me and cares for my every need.

All Good Men

Now is the time for all good men to come to the aid
  of their country.
It is high time for all good men (and women) of our
  country to aid in the problems we are having.
It is high time we all get involved in the aiding (praying
  for) our country before it falls.
There are no absolutes in the carnal world. There are
  absolutes in God's world. Right is right. Wrong is
  wrong. Black is black and white is white. There is
  no grey.
Where are all the good men who care about right and
  wrong? Where are all the good women who care?
  Where are all the good people of this country who
  really care about where we are headed?
When will we be so concerned that we take action
  against the wrong in our country? When will we be
  willing to act on our convictions? Stand for what is
  right? Speak out? (or support those who do)
Now is the time to act and speak. Now is the time to come
  to the aid of our country.

"all the glory"

Who shall be praised? Who deserves honor?
Who is blessed with beauty?

What can match the splendor of the sky?
    of the mountains?
The glory of the Lord is a call to rejoice!
He is Light in all His glory!

There is nothing we can do that is worthy
    of glory.
All our talents, beauty and provisions are
    blessings from God.
He is the giver of all good gifts.

TO ALL SOLDIERS SERVING THEIR COUNTRY:

In **Psalms 91** are some verses that might give you comfort:

Verse 4: The Promise of Protection – "He shall cover you with His feathers, and under His wings shall you trust and find refuge; His truth and His faithfulness shall be your shield and buckler."

Verse 7 & 8: The Promise of Safety – "A thousand shall fall at your side and ten thousand at your right hand; but it will not come near you. You will only watch with your eyes as you witness the reward of the wicked."

Verse 11 & 12: The Promise of Help – "For He will give His angels charge over you, to keep you in all your ways. They will lift you up in their hands, lest you dash your foot against a stone."

Our prayers go with you.
May God hold you in the palm of His hands.

'In the Heat of Battle'

Do we fight?
Do we run?
Do we hide?
Do we rationalize "Why the heat?"
Do we make excuses?
Do we stand before the firing squad willingly?
Do we divert the enemies' attention?

We must make the most of every opportunity to advance.
We must move back from the front lines.
We must dodge bullets during our retreat.
We must be alert, for we know not who our enemy is
    (no matter the name, it is Satan).
We must clear our minds, use discernment and make
    proper decisions—our very future is at stake!

The battle rages on . . . .

HIS LOVE

Your Love For Me

No matter what comes my way, I feel your love every day.
The peace you give is like the freshness of spring.
I can soar to heights I've never known without delay.
Joy and comfort you bring to me. You give me a song to sing.

In your presence there is freedom to be the person I should be.
Your words are kind; no one fills me like you.
Without you I am lost. Don't you see?
There is no one who loves me like you do.

```
Whenever I feel discouraged,

whenever I feel depressed,

You are my strength and my buckler.

You are my peace and rest.

No other can offer me comfort,

when trouble may come my way.

I praise You for grace and mercy.

That covers me all of my days.
```

My Lord

My Lord, you are so awesome.
I see your love for me each day.
You guide my feet so faithfully.
No one else can lead me home.
I have put my trust in you alone.
Keep me in the shelter of your wing.
You have proven your watch over me.
From your presence I never want to roam.

Guide me.
Shelter me.
Lead me.
Keep me.

I See the Lord

I see the Lord, in the green spring grass.
I see the Lord in the cattle on the neighbor's
pasture.
I see the Lord in the squirrel scurrying up the
tree.
I see the Lord surrounding the warriors in Iraq
and around the world.
The Lord is present in every good thing.
The beauty of the Lord is round about us.
The Lord is a shield of protection around us.

"into my presence"

"Come into my presence," says the Lord.
"Enjoy my sweet company.
You can dine with me.
I will give you a place to lay your weary head/body.
We will converse—just the two of us—about the revelations all
mankind really wants to hear and know."

I've strayed so far from you, Lord.
My heart has waxed hard and cold.
Wash me, Dear Lord; clean my heart, I pray.
Show me your will for me, each and every day.

As I Walk . . . . .

As I walk, let me walk close to You.
Direct my steps in the path You would have me trod.
May my days be filled with the pleasure of Your company.
When I stumble and fall, hide me in the safety of Your arms.
In my travels, show me the way to fulfill my longing for Your love.
Give me discernment for choosing the direction of every day.
Guide my path that it may be Your will I finally achieve.
As I falter, show me the way You would have me go.
May I never be so discouraged as to quit.
Thank You for Your watch over me.
Praise You for Your care.
You fulfill me
as I walk.

155

"The Lord Speaks"

What can I do for you, saith the Lord so sweetly?
How can I make you trust me more?
I can fill your life so completely.
Tenderness for one another I can restore.
Your life is short and full of some gladness, trouble and trials.
Lean on me, my dear child. Trust me each day.
Your travels will be secure and happy over the coming miles.
I will hold you in the palm of my hands and show you the way.

OPEN MY EYES

I need your direction for my life.
It seems any purpose has gone from me.
I feel so unworthy of your love.
I can never repay what I owe to you.

Give me your peace and security once more.
Let me know you are still caring for me.
Lift my spirit to look toward you.
Remind me of your eternal purpose for my life.

Open my eyes that I may see the truth you have for me.
Open my heart that I may feel love for those around me.
Open my arms to respond with a hug of love to others.
Open my mind to new revelations from you each day.

You have rescued my life.

He Shelters and Restores

Where is God amidst the heartache and trouble of life?
He is present through all the pain and strife.
When parents part, where is the presence of God?
He is guarding the children with every step their feet trod.

When a loved one is laid to rest, He is close by our side.
He dries our tears and gives us a peace, as in His love we abide.
In sickness, He's our comfort and He brings sweet rest.
Under the shelter of His wing, we'll have the strength to pass any test.

With loss of job or profession, He channels us in a new direction.
Constant prayer and submission bring any situation into correction.
There are no mistakes with God. He knows what is ahead.
If we align ourselves with Him, there is a victory in our future instead.

As He watches over the sparrow, He clothes and feeds it, you see.
Then, how much more does He care for you and me?
Not a concern goes unseen. Not a tear goes unnoticed by our Lord.
To the believer, life and a purpose to us can surely be restored.

Carry Your Cross

Carry your cross over hill and vale.
Carry it over rough, rocky roads.
Carry it amongst confusion and uncertainty.
Hang onto it when the strong winds blow.
Don't let it slip away with in torrents of rain.

What is your Focus?

Are you focusing on the eternal or the worldly?
Pray without ceasing, for His will to be done in your life.
Pray while washing dishes, watching football,
or driving your car.

Are you scattered here and there with today's worries?
Listening for God's voice every moment is priceless.
Every thought or deed planted on rocky soil is lost.

Are you praying for God's will in your life?
Catch the inspiration He has for you.
Be still and know that He is God.

"I want to know what I am really all about.
I want Him to be my focus in life.
I want to hear from Him."

"in the center of His will"

Where does God want me to be? Am I listening to His voice?
　Is He calling me to places unknown? Or to work where I am?
What is His will for my life?

May I be found listening, ready to go, willing to stay, or do whatever
　He guides me through.
May He close doors and open those which lead to His perfect will
　for my life.
May I be able to endure whatever hardships or heartaches are
　necessary while enroute to the will of the Father for my life.

Ocean Waves

As I stood at the shore, with the waves lapping at my feet,
　it was as if they were coming in to cleanse me,
　then carry the dirty water out to sea.
The continual touch of the waves on the sand left a
　contentment in my heart.
Even though the waves will return to continually wash
　me, I cherished that moment of cleansing.
Those thoughts purified my mind of present cloudiness.
Only the pebbles can produce the cleansing my soul requires.
The sandy water must penetrate every crevice to truly cleanse
　me. Purify my heart, O Lord.

159

A new beginning

Each day is a new beginning.
The sun will come up in the morning.
Remember the dream god has given you.
Don't let it fade as evening draws nigh.
Tomorrow brings new hope and possibilities.

Don't look back

Look to the future with great anticipation.
The past is done and unable to be retrieved.
Keep your eye on your goal with thanksgiving.

Jesus, I love you. I know thou art mine.
All my life I will praise you. You are all divine.
How can I thank you for what you've done for
me?
When I need a friend, you are there. None other
can I see.
You are worthy of all glory, honor and praise.
I will love and thank you all of my days.

Help me, Lord, your will to do, I pray.
Show me the steps to take each and every day.
I can accomplish nothing without you.
I want to be a witness, tried and true.

Which One Should I Pick?

MAX

You were an orphan, but you found a wonderful home.
Kyla & Jim loved you, so you never wanted to roam.
You stayed alone in a cage for 12 hours—without making a mess!
You even 'sat,' 'laid down' and 'rolled over' to have your paws wiped.
You passed every test!
You loved your new country home and the freedom you found there.
You were so happy that with the neighbors special greetings you did share.
Your eyes told it all, Max.
They revealed an understanding and a kindness that was true.
Even Shadow must have known the kind of friend he had in you.
You were loved by all your family and friends.
Our love and respect for you will *never, never* end!

--from hash to heaven . . . . .

Our Sweet Tanner

Tanner is a special dog. There is no other canine like her.
She has moved from place to place, wherever her family did go.
A bone is taken so gently from any hand, yes sir.
Tanner is loyal to those who love her, with politeness to show.

She watches over the children and follows them from here to there.
When we wave goodbye, she waves to us with her tail.
Tanner seems to know our intent and trusts us without despair.
Running is what she loves to do. Escorting us, she will prevail.

163

Pick of the Litter

"Which one should I pick, Daddy?" asked his daughter,
while selecting a puppy of her very own.
The final selection was the puppy who came to the little girl
because he wanted to.
The "pick of the litter" may be the prettiest, the smartest,
the friendliest, or he might possess the best physique
or personality.
This concept not only applies to puppies, but to people.
To take your pick based on any one of the above qualities
may not necessarily be the best choice. It all depends
on your perspective.
CHOOSE WISELY!

Our Cat, Jerry

You would like our cat, Jerry.
He follows along in front of you, his food to see.
He is affectionate and loving, too.
But he is not crazy about tuna. How about you?
In the warm garage, he will stay on his soft bed.
The deer hunters come and Jerry from the shed does fled.
When the cows need hay, he is curious and will go along for fun.
Exploring he goes for a few days, but we hope back home he will always come.

Clues for the
Miscellaneous
And
Custom Poetry

Treasure Hunt Clues

Group #1
1. Birds fly NORTH in the spring. Find their house and do your thing!
2. Your next clue is on the "big old log." Hop on over, jiggety-jog!
3. The doghouse in the pen is the place to go. Watch out for all our dogs, don't you know?
4. The gas tank holds your next clue, Hop on over. That's what you should do!
5. You have completed your Easter Capers! In the garage, you'll find the IMPORTANT PAPERS!

Group #2
1. Birds fly SOUTH in the winter. Find their house, but don't get a splinter!
2. Go on over to the bird feeder, if it's feed you need. You'll find your clue near the keeper of the seed.
3. You'll find your next clue on the "crawl-space door." Hurry folks! There's much more.
4. Go to the big Rock and you will see what the next clue has in store for thee!
5. You have completed your Easter Capers! In the shed, you'll find the IMPORTANT PAPERS!

--Give the first clue to the 'captains' of Groups 1 and 2.
Place the remaining clues on their respective places.

Bridal Shower Invitation Examples:

If you have a china teacup, sitting in your cabinet,
collecting dust.
you could bring it to the shower.
To Jill's collection, it will adjust.
Maybe a trip to an antique store is in order,
for the cup and saucer, too.
Money is not the object. The teacup would be nice,
but mostly,
it's just having you!

****

If you have a china teacup sitting in your cabinet, all alone.
bring it to Jill's shower. In her teacup collection,
it will find a new home.
A trip to an antique store may be in order,
for the cup and saucer, too.
It's not spending lots of money that counts.
It's your love for Jill, maybe a teacup,
but mostly—it's having the company of you!

A Marriage Recipe

It takes many gifts of love to make a marriage grow.
Forgiveness, trust, and patience are just a few, you know.

My hand-written recipes are those that I use all the time.
I'm sharing them with you—to your kitchen from mine.

In a recipe several ingredients are needed to
complete the task at hand.
A happy marriage is the union of the ideal
lady and her man.

(or)

A Marriage Recipe

My hand-written recipes are those that I use all the time.
I'm sharing them with you—to your kitchen from mine.

Even though the recipe card is not always the final say,
You may add or subtract in any way.
Just like Grandma, not a recipe did she go by,
but her cooking was unbelievable—oh my!

It takes several ingredients to create that special dish.
And I'm hoping for you the greatest recipe of marriage
will be my best wish.

CUSTOM POETRY
By Karen

Need a gift for someone who has everything? How about an original poem?

For that special someone who is dear to your heart,
Try a Custom Poem by Karen for a great start!

Give me the facts about the person for the poem, please.
I'll put them together with style and perfect ease.

The facts can be such items as characteristics and accomplishments, too.
Add some experiences, fun times, likes, dislikes—to be rhymed for you.

Twenty-five dollars a poem will be the charge.
The prose may be serious, funny, small or large.

Give me a call at (217) 882-2110, or email me at
ksmc88@irtc.net now.

Your poem will be a unique gift, and how!

Have your "special" poem framed. You'll have a gift your friend will not forget!

Treat someone on their birthday, anniversary, or give a tribute to a deceased loved one.